Last Words : Broadsheets 1970-1980

Oswald Mosley

Last Words : Broadsheets 1970-1980
Oswald Mosley

Copyright © 2019 Sanctuary Press Ltd

All rights reserved. No part of this book may be reproduced in any form by any electronic or mechanical means including photocopying, recording, or information storage and retrieva without permission in writing from the publisher.

ISBN-13: 978-1-913176-10-5

Sanctuary Press Ltd
71-75 Shelton Street
Covent Garden
London
WC2H 9JQ

www.sanctuarypress.com
Email: info@sanctuarypress.com

Introduction

Oswald Mosley was possibly the most controversial politician of the twentieth century. Many believe he was the greatest thinker of his age, he was certainly the finest orator of his generation.

After service in the Royal Flying Corps in the First World War, he entered parliament determined to ensure good jobs and decent homes for all. He became a Minister in the Labour Government with a special responsibility for ending unemployment. When that Government refused to act he resigned forming first the New Party and later the British Union of Fascists. In the latter he devised policies to create full employment through a British Corporate State and more effective government through an Occupational Franchise.

Mosley was almost alone in opposing the Second World War with his policy of 'Peace with Honour, Empire Intact and British People Safe.' For speaking against that War, which was to cost 60-million lives, Mosley and over 1000 of his most active followers were imprisoned without charge or trial in 1940.

After the War Mosley was back. He formed the Union Movement with a new policy of 'Britain First in Europe a Nation'. His concept of a United Europe was light years ahead of contemporary thinking on European unity and his version is still considered by many to be far superior to the European Union of today.

In 1966 Mosley withdrew from party warfare to advance his ideas by other means: numerous interviews and debates on television and radio followed.

Introduction

In the last decade of his life, Mosley produced the series of Broadsheets contained in this book. These were sent to supporters, opinion formers and people of influence across the world. In these remarkable texts he combined intellect with experience as he turned his attention to the problems of recession, irresponsible banking, mass immigration, exploitation of Third World peoples as cheap labour, the global rise in food and energy prices and unrelenting armed conflict throughout the world.

If the problems sound familiar, Mosley's solutions contained in these Broadsheets most certainly won't.

"Where is the enthusiasm of a great campaign to reveal the real choice between reversion to an isolated, beleaguered island, and rapid advance to a complete European democracy?" – The Mosley Broadsheets.

Jeff Walder

1

Britain's European Policy

LIKE two runaway trains without drivers, two bureaucracies approach a head-on collision in Britain's negotiations to enter the Common Market. The reason is that the London and Brussels officials in recent years have had no effective political direction, and consequently lack clear policies which could avert the crash.

Meanwhile many British people have been sufficiently bemused to turn against the whole idea by the untrue tale that their fellow Europeans have rebuffed them. In fact no-one has kept them out except their own politicians. It was Eden who said Britain's entry into Europe was "something we know in our bones we cannot do", and Bevin who refused the first steps toward the Common Market by turning down the Schumann Plan for a European Coal and Steel Community. A combination of both parties tried to straddle the diverse stools of America, Commonwealth and Europe with the inevitable result of falling between the three. On the other hand, de Gaulle, after this whole experience and after British governments' plain preference for America in all serious matters, still affirmed in one of his last press conferences that he would welcome Britain with all his heart when the British became Europeans. After his departure we face the facts without the alibi, as was said in the last French presidential election.

It is a serious situation because almost all informed opinion at last recognises that Europe is essential to Britain's future. We need the large and assured market, and in the modern world we also require industries built on a continental scale. Moreover, the loss of an Empire leaves a deep psychological necessity for a great people again to play a great part in the world. All this awaits the British in an equal partnership of the European peoples with full scope for their political and technological genius. Yet they are inhibited by a combination of umbrage and apprehension, huff and fear, quite unworthy of our people.

Can it be true that the British in a club of equals will so far fail to hold their own that they will lose their whole identity? Does Britain feel it can no longer produce statesmen capable of persuading other peoples to accept our ideas? This instinct to withdraw like a snail into the brittle shelter of its own little shell is indeed a striking contrast to the spirit of the men who went out looking for trouble and picked up an Empire.

The live alone complex is of course camouflaged in grandiloquent language. An independent Britain is expected to beat the world by selling over 30 per cent of its manufactures on overseas markets in face of intensified competition. When it comes down to practical details we hear talk of using a floating exchange rate to give our exports particular advantages. This was the centrepiece of the Birmingham proposals for which I was responsible in the twenties.

This unorthodox suggestion for exchange manipulation was dismissed at the time as youthful impudence by the deadheads who say during the first half of life that you are too young and the second half too old, to do anything; by which they mean they are always against anything being done. The difference in the present situation is that everyone has at length rumbled this economic trick, and is inclined to try the same game. If we succeeded in making ourselves nuisance enough for long enough on world markets our goods might face total exclusion from the developing continental systems. At best this device is a temporary expedient until we get into Europe.

Resistance to Common Market entry rests on a massive misunderstanding of the facts, past and present, which does not surprise me after living and travelling in Europe during the past twenty years. Experience of the different traditions and methods of the European peoples assists in devising new policies—large and strong enough to avert the coming collision between two systems—by lifting thought and action to a new level. For example, Britain runs its agriculture with only 3 per cent of its working population on the land. This efficiency is gained at the expense of being a top heavy island with most of its population living and working in the towns. Other European nations take a different view of their national requirements and security; consequently they have large populations of comparatively small farmers who have lived for centuries in more sheltered and self contained systems.

Therefore at the start of negotiations the two bureaucracies face the dilemma, either that Britain pays a lot to maintain continental agriculture or that Europeans must suddenly change their way of life. In practice, this means adopting the Mansholt Plan which would rapidly remove over five million European farmers from the land and place them either in the employment of the towns or in their unemployment queues. It is difficult to conceive a more dangerous procedure in the present world situation. So the trouble is that Britain risks paying too much, or Europe risks blowing up.

This is the moment for Britain to enter with big policies, not small haggles. Napoleon called us a nation of shopkeepers, and our politicians sometimes make us look like a nation of shoplifters. Let us instead take the lead in creative ideas. Why reduce food production throughout Europe and drive millions from the land, while many more millions in the third world starve? Bring the Dominions and America into a comprehensive plan to end starvation on earth, and carry the cost of full agricultural production on a combined budget. Gradual rationalisation of farming should mean more, not less production. We must raise the sights of policy and together solve the related problems of world hunger and of Western agriculture. It is time to stop quarrelling, and to start thinking.

2

Inflation and Depression – The Worst of Both Worlds

ARE economists people who cannot see the wood for the trees? They have recently been preoccupied with the circumstances prevailing since the last war, and with the ingenious technical devices which they believed would make this special situation last forever. The western world was assured that their "built-in stabilisers" would certainly prevent recurrence of anything like the depression of the thirties. The truth is that the real problem is too large for these small adjustments.

May I attempt a clear analysis in layman's language? My opinion has at least the weight of a man who committed his political life to the disturbing belief that sooner or later an economic crisis of this basic nature was inevitable, and to his view of the drastic measures necessary to meet it. Situations like the "great slump" can recur if nothing effective and durable is done to remove their deep causes, and nothing constructive and permanent has been done.

Economic crisis was postponed by a second world war, preceded and followed by armament booms. Then came the cold war, accompanied by two small hot wars in Korea and Vietnam. Throughout this period the world-wide rivalries and hostilities of the American and Soviet systems have incurred vast expense on earth and in space with immense demands on industrial output. Yet despite this ready-made market for the constantly increasing production of modern science the western-world has been continually threatened with the return of depression. The basic difference at present is inflation. Previously prices, employment and the stock exchanges all fell together. Now employment and the stock exchanges fall, while prices rise. Thus we confront the worst of both worlds, rising prices and a falling economy. The reason is that the present rulers of the western world have chosen an initially easier but ultimately even more disastrous policy. They have permitted and encouraged the illusions of inflation rather than face the real challenge of recession.

A sick man often does not feel the full effects of a dangerous illness while fever lasts. The end of fever is the beginning of recovery, but at that moment he feels much worse. We should not think much of a doctor who does nothing or little to stop a fever because he fears the bad temper of the patient when it ends. Yet this is exactly the conduct of politicians who permit inflation because they fear the electoral consequences of depression. Instead of facing the situation with real remedies—which must now be drastic and unpleasant—they allow the continuance of inflation to postpone the day of political reckoning. Things are made no better if the doctor runs a circus instead of a hospital.

Inflation accelerates when people lose faith in the value of money and begin to convert cash into goods. We suffer from a modern and complex variant of an old disease. The last conspicuous example was Germany in the twenties, when a sackful of bank notes was needed to buy the family dinner. A disaster of this degree is of course unlikely to occur in two continents. Yet the underlying tendency is similar and its consequences can be considerable. Lenin and Keynes at least agreed that inflation is the recipe for revolution. The attempt to postpone economic depression with the fatal device of a general inflation is bad enough. This is now complicated by a cost-push inflation within the demand inflation. Not only have we too much money chasing too few goods, but the lion's share of the available money is grabbed by the strong trade unions whom government fears. As usual the lion is followed by the jackal of speculation to lick up any remaining profits of inflation. The general public is left with both the cost and the push: high prices and unemployment.

Inflation and Depression - The Worst of Both Worlds

We need government strong enough to represent the nation in face of trade union and money power. The first task is to stop the general demand inflation. Stripped of technical jargon, this means that the supply of money shall not exceed the supply of goods. Neither for purpose of its own overspending, nor for other purposes of industry, must government allow cash to outstrip production. This would involve unemployment, because no administration in recent times has managed to maintain stable prices without unemployment. Government must therefore act to provide public works for the unemployed; works which can be both permanent, revenue earning national assets, and a long overdue clean-up of Britain to include the end of slums and pollution.

These measures would be out of the question in an inflationary situation because they would add to the inflation. Public works could however be a remedy for the temporary depression caused by the end of the inflation, and could then be financed without undue difficulty; it is now generally agreed that the plan I devised for this purpose in the government of 1930 would have been effective. The large majority do best with stable prices, steady employment and wages which increase with growing production. Yet this situation causes the unemployment of a small minority, and they should not be penalised by compulsory idleness.

The next duty of government, elected by the whole people, is to give effective economic leadership. It alone should govern in economics as in other spheres. This does not mean constant control or fussy interference in the affairs of industry. It does mean that government must give a lead in deciding the main questions of wages and prices, and should ask parliament for compulsory powers when necessary. We recently experienced some negative action to which politicians were driven by the logic of events, but then came retreat under trade union pressure. We have never yet had the positive use of a wage-price mechanism, which I first suggested fifteen years ago. Certainly government should consult every interest in serving the good of all, but in the life and death question of economic survival government must decide and act.

3

A Speech to the Conservative Bow Group

THE main obstacle to Britain uniting with the rest of Europe was the widespread belief that the British people were not Europeans at all. It was felt that they were making belated application to join for purely material reasons, and that their preoccupation with their narrow and selfish interests would make them more nuisance than they were worth. It was necessary that this blunt truth should be stated by an Englishman who had lived in Europe long enough to know the facts.

This deep European suspicion of Britain's motives was reinforced by the present swing of British opinion against joining Europe. The change of feeling was due to the total failure of the parties to explain the facts and to arouse any enthusiasm among our people for a supreme opportunity to our country. They had failed either to argue the case with the force of necessity or to inspire it with the ideal.

Union with Europe should be treated as launching a crusade, not as opening a bazaar. It was idle to advance toward the greatest achievement of 3,000 years of European history with music which Bernard Shaw would have described as "the funeral march of a fried eel". To convince that we were Europeans we needed to feel and show some passion, some sense of the greatness of European destiny.

It was unworthy of the British people to be represented by their politicians as a row of small shopkeepers trying to turn a quick penny, or a man sidling into a prosperous community to pick a pocket. Certainly we should seek economic advantage, but

A Speech to the Conservative Bow Group

we should achieve it in building the prosperity of all to which British science, technology and political genius could make an immense contribution.

It had long been evident that mass production for an assured market was the only basis for industrial survival in the modern world. It was also the only means to secure an overall system of low prices. Yet we were asked to reject this opportunity in case we suffered an increase in the price of butter. Would our people refuse to win a war when national survival was involved, for fear of an increase in the price of butter? The issues now facing us were just as grave for our future.

It was also now evident that modern industry in the new scientific age could only be developed with the related resources of an entire continent. Those who talked of a small island going alone in a free world market took no account of modern machines. Their only mechanical requirement was a Time Machine to take them back to the 19th century. Subsequent development of science had reinforced his view of 20 years ago: "Science leaves us with only one choice — union with Europe."

The development of the large technical civilisations had also divided Britain from the Dominions which were now dependent both economically and militarily on America. Yet in cooperation a united Europe and the Dominions could develop policies of an altogether different scale both in industry and agriculture. Europeans at home and overseas could together solve their agricultural problem by deciding at last to feed the hungry of the world, and to carry the cost on a combined budget. The ideal and the practical could unite in an act both of charity and of real policy. The making of Europe was no small thing, and in the end it would be found that we could only do great things in a great way.

The case for European union was now reinforced by the American retreat from its world role. Those who had lived happily but ignobly under American protection might soon have to look after

Last Words : Broadsheets 1970-1980

themselves. Not only the whole basis of American political and military strategy but also the American dream had been shattered, when the war begun by President Kennedy at the age of 44 had been won by President Ho Chi Minh at the age of 79.

Disaster had hit America through ignoring the elementary facts of life, which British soldiers had known since their original Irish experience half a century ago. Political guerrillas supported by a courageous civilian population could always baffle a regular army, particularly when it was as alien as a Western army on the Asian mainland. That was why - "hold Europe: leave Asia" - had seemed to him the only realistic policy since 1950.

These same dangers could threaten their European homeland in time of economic crisis. To believe that the Channel was any longer a protection either from nuclear rockets or from revolutionary politics was just to put the head under the bedclothes. Britain could not escape its destiny in a world of dark danger but of glittering opportunity, and in a great age must resolve again to play a great part.

4

The Reorganisation of Government

A START has been made with the long overdue reorganisation of government - a matter of vital interest to the whole nation. "Even the ranks of Tuscany could scarce forbear to cheer", particularly when old opponents adopt policies presented long ago. A power house of government in Downing Street was a proposal of my resignation speech in 1930, and was reiterated with additions in "My Life" 1968, only to be implemented during 1970 in a form emasculated rather by lack of executive dynamism than of political process. The time-lag is only 40 years - congratulations! - if we keep moving we may yet catch the bus for Europe.

Government is reorganised, but where is the power to act? Government action is chiefly needed in the sphere of wages, prices and the support or rather the leadership of modern science and technology. Yet government has specifically renounced the right to act in an incomes policy, and the direct relationship between the Downing Street power house and science is diffused through a multi-functional Ministry. It is useless to reorganise government without power or plan to act; "all dressed up and nowhere to go."

First, clarity is needed on the function of government, which is presently the subject of much confused thinking. The modern State rests precariously between two absurdities. On the one extreme is continual interference by government to teach industrialists their own business. This tendency reached its farcical culmination in the scene described by the Brown memoirs, when a grandiose scheme for the supercession of the Treasury in favour of an improvised economic and financial panjandrum called DEA was launched during a few light words

Last Words : Broadsheets 1970-1980

in a taxicab; shades of MacDonald and Thomas, "plus ca change, plus c'est la meme chose."

On the other extreme is the 19th century concept of a free market economy in which government has little to do except levy taxes and keep order, until it finally breaks down because "to hell with the foreigners" has prevented entry into any wider economy which can provide market and industrial relations adequate to the needs of modern technology. Life in government can be equally easy-oozy, in the old MacDonald phrase, either in the hurried taxi-colloquies or in the armchair of high principled inactivity which only requires between yawns the occasional emission of a trite little classroom aphorism with an air of Delphic wisdom.

Real life is not so simple; we need a view of government at once more balanced and more dynamic. Inflation must be stopped, and this means power not only to act on demand-pull inflation by monetary and fiscal measures, but also on cost-push inflation by statutory authority for government to prevent the exploitation of wage demands by the strong trade unions or of the price racket by strong financial interests. It means power to lead the economy by a positive and not merely negative incomes policy, if the brain drain is to be stopped, merit rewarded, and the rule of grab ended.

Much more could be done at once by fiscal measures within the national capacity to save the able and the needy, the salaried managers of industry and the unorganised and therefore underpaid, the considerable mass of the still poor and the old. Abolish surtax on earned income; far more effective as incentive than spreading the jam over all the bread with sixpence off income tax. But this real encouragement for initiative must be balanced by far more real compassion for the poor and defenceless.

The reorganisation of government is not enough if what we call firm decisions and the Americans call agonising reappraisals are lacking. The Ministry to deal with environment is a fine concept, but see the large decisions this involves. Is a part of the resources allocated to growth—which is becoming a fetish—now to be transferred to the rebuilding of slums and the end of pollution? The same great decision could stop inflation and save environment. Really stopping inflation will inevitably cause unemployment and temporary depression. This will be the chance both to get the economy moving again on healthier and more rational lines and for a direct attack by government on the housing problem and pollution. It will in effect be a temporary and beneficent transfer of resources from growth to environment. It will need courageous decision because both employment and the question of industrial investment for future growth will arise. Steady employment in a stable price level and consequent conditions of confidence for capital investment can be the benefit of a successful operation, but it is idle to believe that the process will be neither severe nor painful. Government must show the same courage which is often asked of an individual, facing a short bad time to win a long good time.

Facts will soon impose more and larger decisions on trade union legislation. The modern fact is that power has passed from the trade union office to the shop floor. The individual wants his say in the practical affairs of everyday life as well as in a vote every four years, and he often feels with reason that he has a more valuable contribution to make in this new industrial democracy. This was a tendency recognised in my writings on "European Socialism" during the fifties and in much contemporary European thinking, but has yet to be recognised by British government.

The real task of government is in the forbidden sphere of wages and prices and in the encouragement of science. It is not to control or direct the daily affairs of industry but to lead it in enterprises too large for private enterprise. Government should precede industry like a bulldozer going through the jungle of impediments, and also should protect industry and the individual from the dangers of the present jungle economy, the monopoly powers of trade union and finance which have long rendered derisory any concept of the free market. The life determining affairs of scientific research and development are often too large for individual industries; they were led with extraordinary results by American government for purposes of war and can be led by government with the combined resources of Europe to secure the safety of our civilisation and the wealth and happiness of our people.

5

Inflation - Employment - Incomes Policy

To Simplify Truth is the Art of Politics

THE Prime Minister in a recent broadcast invited definition of an incomes policy from anyone still bold enough to hold a plan rejected by the present government and fled from by the last. I first advanced such a policy fifteen years ago,[1] long before politicians were driven toward it by the logic of events and away from it by pressure of sectional interests. The positive use of a wage-price mechanism by government seemed to me the necessary beginning to any answer of our economic problem. It has never yet been tried in a statutory or even in a voluntary form, because a wage freeze is the reverse of an active policy; a negative is not a positive, the petrified is not the dynamic.

It is of course evident that no incomes policy will work without corresponding monetary and fiscal measures. A prime example of current confusion in thinking is the presentation of incomes policy as an alternative to monetary restraint. Any serious attempt to deal with inflation clearly requires both. A demand-pull inflation will always cause prices to rise if the money supply exceeds equivalent production, whatever the incomes policy. Excessive wage increases extorted by powerful trade unions will always cause unit costs to rise in a cost-push inflation, whatever the monetary policy. We need clear, firm policies in each case.

The truth should also be stated that to stop inflation will cause unemployment. To pretend otherwise is to deceive the

1   Detailed definition *Europe: Faith and Plan* 1958.

people. This truth can be supported by clear explanation that a runaway inflation—now in its early stages—can bring a worse unemployment, as well as making worthless the money in pocket or savings. Dismay at the shock of truth can be overcome by the open and vigorous preparation of public works to provide useful occupation for the unemployed. It may in the end even prove an advantage for some proportion of manpower to be employed in stopping pollution instead of promoting surplus growth; otherwise the environment problem will never be met. Certainly such measures will be necessary to overcome the temporary depression caused by the end of inflation and to restart the economy. They may even become a long term factor of the economy in view of past evidence that no government has yet succeeded in preventing both inflation and unemployment. Would it really be such a disaster to rebuild the slums and to cleanse the atmosphere instead of making a few more washing machines to put in rotten houses and a few extra cars to poison the air?—even to continue in such a method and spirit? These major changes would present administrative problems of a kind I have encountered successfully in government before. The details must of course be wrestled out within the departments, which provide both the vital aid of complete information and the acid test of ministerial capacity and will. At the political level the main objection must first be met: that growth will stop, new investment will not be forthcoming, and Britain will fall behind in the race for increasingly competitive international markets to which we are condemned by our failure to create a secure base and a stable system in Europe years ago.

It is of course true that through such a policy we should experience the shock of a surgical operation. The question is what would be our subsequent condition? I affirm that a Britain which has stopped inflation and achieved stable prices and conditions of employment will have restored confidence sufficiently to draw capital from all over the world to promote a period of unprecedented growth. If foreign as well as domestic capital is to be used should we not be possessed by foreigners? The answer is that strong government can prescribe the conditions in which foreign money and personnel

Inflation - Employment - Incomes Policy

can come to Britain for good reward in return for good service; if the economy is competitive and therefore healthy we will get all we need on our own terms. It is the weak and not the strong who are possessed; Britain of today, not tomorrow. Some say that harsh facts cannot be stated in a democracy under the parliamentary government to which we all adhere. My own election winning record, when still working within the established system, would suggest the contrary. Today, in gathering evidence of economic crisis, I believe the people can be persuaded to accept necessary truths. For example, a positive use of the wage-price mechanism means that skill and merit in the unusual and unorganised should be fairly rewarded at the same time that the stand and deliver of organised power is checked. Scientists and technicians, doctors and nurses, key skills and devotion must be protected by government asking for power also to secure that they are paid adequately. It is not enough to reply that because they are more scared by what will happen in America than by what is happening in Britain they are now coming home. We cannot build a stable system on the quicksands of panic.

Another vital truth can also become acceptable if clearly stated: a man should be paid what he is worth; in language of the shop floor the rate for the job, a fair differential. What he is worth in simple definition means that he is producing more for the country than he is paid. This is the case of top executives in industry, who should not have their market worth filched away by a state surtax. Such men, and many others in executive and technical positions, do have their worth decided by what industry will pay for their rare services, and this market operation should not be frustrated by penal taxation. It is possible to justify abolishing surtax on earned incomes - bringing an electric impulse of incentive to the nerve centres of industry - if in a wide and deep compassion for the needy the state also truly implements in modern terms the old but often neglected principle that no man shall starve in England. The people can appreciate the basic facts of life if they are clearly and courageously explained, because their own experience and good sense confirm them. To simplify truth is the art of politics.

6

Democracy

Action Within Parliamentary Government

DEMOCRACY either means that the will of the people shall be implemented, or it means nothing. Yet to suggest a system which can, in fact, do what the people want done is often denounced as a denial of democracy, since effective action is regarded as a danger to liberty. In the name of freedom people are condemned to live in slums for fear that a government powerful enough to rebuild the slums might turn life into some kind of prison. Consequently we live in a State of universal negation within a system of individual inhibition.

The individual has liberty to drink or drug himself into oblivion of his inhibitions, but not the liberty to live in a good home easily obtained at a fair rent, or to enjoy a secure livelihood in work which interests him because his ideas are used, while in the evening his enthusiasm is encouraged in an active community life. These things are possible in the age of modern science, but they require organisation on a great scale which means action by government. The failure of government to act results in disillusionment and eventually in the disintegration of society.

Is it possible to reconcile action with liberty? Can we give government power to act and yet make quite certain it will not abuse that power, and will preserve the absolute assurance of individual liberty? I believe we can. Government freely and regularly elected by universal franchise would ask the parliamentary majority to grant it freedom to act in all the main problems facing the nation. It would then be able to do what the people want done, subject to the right of Parliament

Democracy

at any time to dismiss it by vote of censure. Give a man, or in this case a government, a job to do, and sack him if he falls, is a principle most people would support. Commonsense principles of everyday life, which, everyone can understand, are required to cut through the Gordian knot of present confusion and frustration in government.

Members of Parliament should not only have power to dismiss government by a majority vote of censure, but also to question Ministers far more frequently than time now permits. Members of all parties should be attached to each department to make suggestions to Ministers and interrogate them publicly if they proved recalcitrant.

Members of Parliament should also be more closely informed of what is happening in the country by spending more time among their constituents. Time spent in the lobbies or in futile debates would be used instead to share in the daily life and to study the requirements of their constituents. They would then be competent to question Ministers, since they would be well informed by their contacts both with the departments and with the people.

What would be gained and what might be lost by such a reform of government? The gain would be complete freedom to act. For instance, just conceive solving the housing problem by the present rigmarole of interacting procedure between government, Parliament and local authority. The scandal of the slums in Birmingham, Liverpool, Manchester, Glasgow and London itself was one of the main factors which took me into the Labour Party in 1924, after betrayal of the government's pledge in 1918 to rehouse the people with particular reference to the returned ex-servicemen. Yet it was reported in "The Times" of October 22 1969 that 4,500,000 houses still require demolition.

For my part I have proposed ever since return from the war of 1918 that we should solve the housing problem as an "operation of war". Government should mobilise individual firms by mass production methods to build houses as they built ships, planes, shells and mulberry harbours in wartime. When the housing shortage is at length overcome and the slums are rebuilt, industry could revert to private enterprise just as normality returns at the successful conclusion of a war. It would be a national effort to solve a problem which menaces the life, health and happiness of our people. Why should government only have the power to act in time of war; always to destroy, never to build?

The gain in terms of what could be done for our people by this long overdue action of government would be immense. What would be the loss? We should lose whatever advantage is derived from detailed parliamentary debate, an overrated benefit. As an ex-Minister responsible for conducting difficult and complex Bills through Parliament I will not deny there is some benefit. The old adage that several heads are better than one always applies in regarding these measures from all angles in Parliament, because every kind of human and professional experience is to be found there. Yet the real, detailed grilling of the problem by the experts of the departments has already occurred.

The Minister has already accepted valuable advice and made his own contribution if he is any good, and his job in Parliament is more by debating skill and agreeable manners to get the Bill through prolonged and successive readings as quickly as possible. Members of Parliament lacking the mass of detailed information which is only available in the departments are tempted instead to obstruct with party politics. We never learn all the facts until we become Ministers; that is why all party programmes are more or less bogus.

The task of the Minister is to grasp the facts available in the department, and to decide his action; it should, of course, coincide with and not contradict the party statement of intent at the previous election. If he knows his own mind and comes to clear decisions he will be supported by the complete loyalty of the Civil Service. The elaborate paraphernalia of detailed Parliamentary discussion dates from a previous epoch, and today wastes time without really touching more than the fringe of the subject. My old gag about government and opposition—fancy running a factory by paying one man to do a job and another man to stop him —was demagogic, but contained an element of truth.

Admittedly Ministers would lose some time in dealing with all-party committees to co-operate with the departments, but nothing like the time they now waste in hanging about the lobbies day and night in idle discussion. Also there would be a corresponding gain in learning continually what was happening in the country from M.P.s who were in close and constant touch with their constituents. My wish that "Governments should always know what the people are thinking, and the people should always know what the government is doing", would then be implemented. The Prime Minister would find it worthwhile to see these committees at regular intervals and to learn the facts of daily life. He would also do well to inform and be informed by often submitting himself to interrogation before television by skilled journalists armed with all the facts of their organisations. That would be the beginning of "participation".

For the rest, effective participation surely entails the consultation of every man in his daily work, above all the careful study of any idea he presents for its improvement, and opportunity to enter in an organised form into all questions affecting his daily community life at home. This is an interest which has occupied me from the co-partnership and profit-sharing schemes of the twenties to the "European Socialism" —briefly, syndicalism in industries now nationalised—which I was suggesting in the fifties. It was inherent, too, in my proposals for an occupational franchise in the thirties. I do not, at present, advocate this reform, because such great changes will be necessary before long to overcome economic crisis that we should undertake nothing which is not strictly necessary; we should say with Jeremy Bentham: "minimise pain". What matters is that full outlet to every man's mind and spirit in work and daily life shall be secured in this mechanical age.

Last Words : Broadsheets 1970-1980

Can we then agree that democracy consists firstly in government with the duty and the power to do what the people have elected it to do, subject not only to their will at frequent multiparty elections but also to instant dismissal at any time by their elected representatives, and secondly in the organised consultation of the whole people in their work and daily life In a manner so thorough and systematic that it can only be initiated and conducted under the auspices of the government they have elected for this purpose? If we can agree that some such measures can give the people effective control over their internal affairs and lives, we are still faced with the problem how they can change the present control of their country by external factors. It is not much good taking all this trouble to manage our own affairs, if they can be completely upset any day by some outsider.

What Mr, Attlee used to call "external factors" have continuously wrecked the best laid plans of social democrat governments both in Britain and Europe. We depend at present not only on the vagaries of world markets but on control by foreign bankers who dictate to British government the necessary measures to maintain our balance of payments. In this sphere one or other of the weak, divided European countries is always in trouble, because it is self-evident that all countries cannot simultaneously sell more than they buy. The resultant movements from surplus into deficit and back into surplus are ordained by foreign bankers: we live under a system of external financial control. What nonsense in these circumstances to talk of the sovereignty of the nation or its people, or even to maintain that democracy exists. We are governed not by the vote of the people but by dictates from abroad, and in a Eurodollar world by inflation partly imported from abroad.

It is necessary to unite with the rest of Europe in order to establish any true basis of democracy. We need not only common market but also common government; I have always contended that to put common market before common government was to put the cart before the horse. We must become a single self-contained country, with no more payments problems within its borders than exists today between Lancashire and Yorkshire. A firm in Manchester may by successful competition put out of business a firm in Lyons or Hamburg—or vice versa, but there will be no national balance of payments problem between Britain, France and Germany. We will never solve these problems or win true independence for the people to rule their own lives by their votes until we have common government and common market; in short, Europe a Nation for which I declared in 1948.

It has long been admitted that to win access to the large and assured market which renders possible modern mass production we must enter a wider economic community. Now it becomes clear to all who seriously study the industrial and technical problem that advanced industries can only be developed with the related resources of an entire continent. I was not far out in the 1940's in saying (1946 and 1947): "The union of Europe becomes not merely a dream or a desire but a necessity" and "Politics must bring in the new world of science to redress the balance of the old world of Europe". European politics, industries and science are becoming completely interwoven, and I maintain again that it was right then to say: "modern statesmen should live and work with scientists as the Medicis lived with artists". They must also live as Europeans and not as mutually suspicious villagers.

What becomes of our national culture and institutions?—the usual misunderstanding arises at this point. Are they really so proud of the roast beef of old England being cooked for ever in Wall Street? Cannot they see that the only way to save our national culture and institutions from the control of foreign bankers, from Americanisation or Soviet domination, is to get together with other Europeans not only to save our whole homeland and make it greater Europe but to preserve our individual cultures within our mutual strength? The combined might of Great Britain never obliged any Englishman to eat haggis or play the bag-pipes, but it did preserve both English and Scottish culture from outside domination for several centuries.

Last Words : Broadsheets 1970-1980

Directly we consider a realistic structure for Europe it is clear that the individual national cultures would be preserved and the control of the people over their own lives would, at length, be established. The government of Europe a Nation should deal only with such questions as foreign policy, defence and the general economic leadership of the whole continent; it would depend on the vote of all the people of Europe for a European Parliament. National Parliaments would also exist as they do today, to deal with all the social and cultural questions of the individual states within Europe. Further devolution to the regions would also be necessary in local parliaments dealing directly with the daily lives of the people. There would be more, not less opportunity than now for the development of local culture. Government can be built in three tiers, the region, the old nation and the new nation. The new nation—Europe a Nation-—would comprise both the regions and the old nations, but would not supersede them. Europe in union alone can give all our peoples the strength and the means to control their own lives and to direct their own destinies. Democracy will then cease to be a sham and become a reality. Our people will enter a wider life of limitless opportunity, in which their political genius may develop to the benefit of all mankind.

7

Confusion in Debate – Inflation and Europe

CONFUSED debates on inflation and Britain's entry into Europe require an attempt at clarity. Mr. Barber condemns inflation but allows an increase in the money supply without any prospect of an equivalent increase in production. Further inflation is thus inevitable, even without a handout budget. He is rightly rebuked on this account by Mr. Powell, who then falls into the elementary error of believing that demand inflation is the sole cause of price rise and that cost inflation does not exist.

Excessive wage exactions by contemporary trade unions can cause price rise in particular industries despite limitations of the money supply. Failing the direct intervention of government with an incomes policy, the only restraint of key trade unions is massive unemployment caused by acute deflation, or the pricing of their products out of export markets; both disastrous. The classroom lucidity of the "Tory tribune", who says these trade unions are "white as snow", might be lifted out of an obsolete pedantry by a more modern study than Irving Fisher's work on quantity theory in 1911, now reflected in the Chicago school of Milton Friedman.

In Europe, British spokesmen appear sadly baffled by the disturbing clarity of the "Latin mind", which has long been regarded in our island as one of the deadly sins. The good European, Mr. Jenkins, was handicapped in his recent television debate by the need for translation to a French audience. Yet a few vague words about all now being interdependent were no answer in any language to M. Couve de Murville's penetrating questions on Britain's attitude within the Common Market in

Last Words : Broadsheets 1970-1980

the event of European interests clashing with external interests. His reply simply confirmed the inhibiting suspicion that Britain enters to turn a quick penny between Europe and America rather than to support or initiate a European patriotism. Mr. Rippon hardly rallied the ranks of Europe with a remark about all being settled after a few more cognacs and coffees, while the French representative was reported to look as if he had just swallowed a lemon. When will our English learn that in serious matters the French are the most deadly serious of European people, and that the affectation of an Elizabethan nonchalance in face of grave events is at present out of place; a Drake played by a duckling is in any case unconvincing.

Seriousness was restored by Professor Kaldor's weighty negative to Europe in the *New Statesman*, which unfortunately remained unanswered in a responsible but inadequate reply by Mr. Lever. This debate is worth examining. Professor Kaldor suggests that Britain should live on world markets by "repeated devaluations". Mr. Lever suggests that we should equip ourselves for expansion and European entry by borrowing from the world with a "marginal increase in inflation". I submit that the third course is to sweat it out on a siege economy with equal sacrifices for all until we are ready to enter Europe "on the right foot". We could combine an "export led economy" with the solution of our environment problem, and could thus save ourselves by our own exertions. We can make ourselves competitive, end inflation and employ those temporarily unemployed in a clean up of Britain which should include rehousing on the scale of an "operation of war". If a united people can make such effort and sacrifice in two wars, why not have the sweat without the blood or too many tears to win our whole future in an economy of limitless potential and a policy of renewed greatness?

The British people are at their best when summoned to a serious effort and convinced there is no alternative. What are the alternatives this time? Mr. Lever would borrow a lot and inflate a little. After the debauch, "a hair of the dog that bit us"; the bright new idea in both America and Britain. To take up the slack in production by a simple expansion of credit was inadequate and dangerous even in the deflationary situation of the twenties; it can be disastrous in the inflationary situation of the seventies. Inflation has never yet cured inflation. Professor Kaldor's main constructive proposal of "repeated devaluations" would surely be more effective in the form of a floating exchange rate. As a temporary device during the initial stages of our entry into Europe I have long supported this measure, but it would no longer work as a permanent solution of our island difficulties.

Our "Birmingham proposals" so long ago as 1925 suggested a floating exchange rate, reinforced by various measures of socialist planning, as a means of survival on increasingly competitive world markets. It could have worked then, but everyone now has rumbled the trick. What in effect are concealed subsidies for exports could easily be countered by others. If we made ourselves nuisance enough for long enough on world markets we should be faced with simple exclusion by the developing continental systems.

There are no short cuts by small, easy paths. The agricultural dilemma will be solved neither by Britain paying too much nor by blowing the ballast out of France and Germany. The Mansholt plan for taking 5 million farmers off the land and placing many of them in the incipient unemployment queues of the towns is a recipe for riot. We must lift agriculture out of this rut by larger policies. Britain should lead in creative ideas such as maintaining full food production, accompanied by the gradual rationalisation of farming, and using the surplus to feed the hungry of the world; a combined plan by America, Europe and the Dominions, jointly financed. We must see the vital connection between phenomena; between the end of inflation and the cleansing of environment, between an agricultural solution and the end of hunger.

To Professor Kaldor my gratitude is due for raising the sights to "fiscal integration", "political union", "a new European nation", as the only final means of making Europe work; a view I have urged for 23 years. His argument on this subject is conclusive, but may not be so popular with those politicians who prefer to enter the water gently with that peculiar sideways, crablike motion which they believe to be the only way of progress for modern Britain. Yet all the economists are at least agreed that the initial difficulties are the problem rather than our final participation "on the right foot" in a technological civilisation whose future is too vast for anyone to quantify. After proving my point that "great things can only be done in a great way", it is a pity that Professor Kaldor should content himself with advocating "frequent devaluations", so familiar in the limited and divisive sphere of South America, so unworkable in the large and unifying sphere of continental systems. Such valuable erudition should not in the end be reduced to two simple propositions—down with Europe, and up with the banana republic.

8
Mosley's Thinking Since the War

IN response to recent interest, the Mosley Secretariat issues the following short summary of some principal points in the post-war thought and writing of Sir Oswald Mosley.

Since 1966 he has acted as an isolated individual, the organisation he founded having since been conducted by other people; vide My Life (1968) and the *New Statesman* (11.12.70).

- "Europe a Nation" (1948). A long advocate of the union of Europe, Mosley has argued that "common market before common government puts the cart before the horse", and he still maintains that effective economic arrangements in Europe require united political action. In particular, he has urged the people of Britain to play a leading part in the creation, with their fellow Europeans at home and overseas, of a new and largely self-contained market and supply system which alone can solve the recurrent trading crises faced by these islands.

- Wage-Price Mechanism (1955) now called "incomes policy". Apparently first in the field with ideas now followed and urged by many leading economists, he has stressed the necessity of Incomes policy for over fifteen years; Galbraith claims to have done so for ten (*New Statesman*, 22.1.71). Detailed exposition appeared in *Europe: Faith and Plan* (1958)

- Guerrilla warfare during nuclear deadlock (European Situation, 1950). His analysis has proved true in Vietnam and elsewhere. Mosley then also argued that urban guerrilla warfare may decide future conflicts; a view now supported by military experts (e.g. General Bethouart, Figaro, 9.3.70).

Last Words : Broadsheets 1970-1980

- Immigration. Mosley first proposed immigration control in 1952 to prevent any problems arising and then suggested that the United Kingdom should have similar rights in this respect as the Dominions. He fought the North Kensington election (1959) on this issue, among others, when the "coloured immigration" problem was of sufficiently manageable proportions to be solved decisively and humanely by economic reconstruction within the Commonwealth. According to Mr. Powell, who was in the government from 1960 to 1963, Britain would not have a serious immigrant problem today "If an Act of Parliament which was passed in 1962 had been passed only five years earlier" (Carshalton, 15.2.71). His Colleague Lord Hailsham wrote: "Mr. Enoch Powell, Minister of Health, was busy importing West Indian nurses to man his hospitals" (*The Spectator* 9.7.69). Responsibility denied.

- Housing as an operation of war. (Mosley Newsletter, 15.11.46). He has consistently proposed that slum-clearance and housing should be treated as a national problem, lifted out of the local authority sphere, and that new homes should be produced as munitions, aeroplanes, ships and mulberry harbours are produced in time of war. Eighteen years later Mr. Wilson said; "Housing must be tackled like a wartime operation. When we needed the guns and tanks ... we mobilized the resources of the country to produce them without regard to private interest or private profit" (*Newsweek*, 28.9.64).

- Union of European and Dominion policies to feed the hungry of the world in conjunction with America (Kensington Town Hall, 25.2.63). These proposals become more than ever relevant in the Common Market agricultural difficulties and resistance to Mansholt plans to uproot millions of peasants from the land and put them in growing urban unemployment queues. Mosley suggested full western agricultural production, using the surplus to end world starvation and carrying the cost on a combined budget.

- Link inflation to environment problem. Quoting Aristotle, Mosley said we need to see the "connection between phenomena not normally apparent"; meaning that to stop inflation will create unemployment, but that the unemployed should be used in dealing with the environment and in other constructive public works long advanced in detailed policy. "It may in the end even prove an advantage for some proportion of manpower to be employed in stopping pollution instead of promoting surplus growth; otherwise the environment problem will never be met" (22.11.70).

- "Hold Europe, leave Asia" (Speech in East London, 11.12.50). Mosley has throughout opposed all western intervention in futile bloodshed on the Asian mainland, and required concentration on the holding of European lands; he contends that Australia can best be defended from Australia. In pursuit of world peace, his chief preoccupation since his service in the First World War, Mosley has advocated that the great powers should maintain different spheres of influence, not for imperialism or aggression, but for aid and guidance, for the non-proliferation of nuclear weapons and for peaceful competition of ideas in genuine coexistence. In addition to America and Russia, Europe, China and Japan, India should be regarded as great power areas of influence and development.

- Science and Government. Their linking together for constructive purposes goes back to his resignation speech (1930) and *The Greater Britain* (1932), but the ideas have been considerably developed in later years. He wrote that statesmen should live "in the company and inspiration of scientists, as a Medici lived in the company and inspiration of artists" (*The Alternative*, 1947).

- Participation. Mosley has urged several social reforms to provide participation and a full life for the individual in modern society. Some of these were outlined in his recent articles in *Eboracum* (York University, 1.12.70) and The *Daily Telegraph Magazine* (29.1.71)

Last Words : Broadsheets 1970-1980

- Personal Liberty. Mosley has proposed a variety of measures to guarantee and extend individual freedom. For example, he has urged a constitutional enactment to prevent imprisonment without trial and a facility whereby maligned individuals or groups can obtain the right to reply in the mass media (*Government of Tomorrow*, 1955).

- "Higher Forms". Mosley has given much thought to the development of a doctrine which can successfully synthesise the deepest traditional values of our civilisation with the biological and technological discoveries of modern science. (Closing pages of *Europe: Faith and Plan*, 1958, and *My Life*, 1968). He has found that in a wider context this thesis often transcends political differences.

9

Forward Into Europe - Not Back to Bretton Woods.

No theme is more sterile for the speaker or repulsive to the audience than I told you so. What matters now is to discuss the constructive alternative to a system that has failed. Is it really necessary to pump the life-blood of a new generation into the dying body of Whig economics? Is world trade the only means of progress, and is commercial division into diverse continental systems really a return to the Dark Ages?

Economists who are unwilling in the light of new facts to discard the traditional wisdom, which some of them found it so difficult to acquire, may still be the men who cannot see the wood for the trees. Practical political commentators, however, begin to identify the basic facts. For example, David Watt in the *Financial Times* (20.8.71) wrote: "Everyone involved wants a balance of payments surplus, and everyone involved wants a slightly undervalued currency ..." It is a pity such a happy state of affairs is impossible by definition". John Graham, Washington correspondent of the same paper, wrote (28.8.71): "One man's surplus is another man's deficit, and this has always been one of the sticking places in the international adjustment process". It was not merely the luck of a controversialist when I said in the previous month during a television debate with Mr. Crossman (28.7.71) "all these little countries are trying at the same time to sell more than they buy, a mathematical impossibility"— since I have been saying this for many years. The surprise is that so many professional economists should have so long failed to recognise the "basic fallacies" on which "rests the precarious structure of the present system" (*Europe: Faith and Plan*, 1958).

Last Words : Broadsheets 1970-1980

The logic of fact and event has at length driven the practical Mr. Nixon in the direction of making an American system. Why is this impossible for a country of such size and resource which is concerned with world trade only to the extent of 4 per cent of its total production? The few supplies it still requires from outside can be easily acquired. The real requirement of America is a policy to equate its vast productive potential with effective home demand. Here again the logic of events drove Mr. Nixon reluctantly toward an Incomes policy which for 16 years I have suggested, not in the negative sense which has alone so far been tried, but as a positive policy for the economic leadership of industry. The wage-price mechanism can and should be used by government for adjusting demand to full production in a system, of stable prices.

The planning of an economy is possible only within a relatively self-contained system, but orthodox economists reject this concept on the ground that production according to local suitability is the only means of rapid progress; consequently any organisation of continental systems is a regression from Bretton Woods, world trade—and world inflation. They ignore the fact that suitability for any particular production can now be created by science in any sphere where raw materials are available, and that the real requirements of progress are size and resource for the development of modern, technological industries combined with a large home market for mass production. America already has this potential, and is being impelled toward its full realisation by the practical sense of its rulers in face of plain facts; only half-hearted measures can destroy it.

Europe is still far from this situation, and fails from lack of will rather than lack of chance. The breakdown of Bretton Woods gives Britain a supreme opportunity to take the initiative in rapid construction of a European system. Fixed parities between European currencies which float against the dollar should be only the prelude to a European currency. Dynamic development of European policies and economics should soon make balance of payments problems between European countries as irrelevant as between Yorkshire and Lancashire. The end of cut-throat competition between them, in which some must always go under, should be followed by the deliberate equation of demand and production through an agreed incomes policy within a continental system. We cannot go back, we must drive hard forward.

Such relatively self-contained continental systems have production and market potential vastly exceeding that of the whole world a few years ago. The full competition of liberal economics can have free play within them, provided there is sufficient dirigisme in central authority through monetary and incomes policy to prevent inflation and to maintain effective demand without disruption from external chaos. Is it really better to refurbish the failed world system of Bretton Woods in which American deficit exported inflation and enabled paper dollars to purchase sound European industries, while European governments rejoiced in their bogus balance of payments surplus supplied by the same American deficit? The taunt that Europeans had not the wit to use the same paper dollars to purchase American industries was cut short by the consequent and inevitable beginning of a runaway inflation in America threatening to wreck the whole crazy merry-go-round.

Even Professor Kaldor's "commodity reserve currency" does not meet the basic dilemma of the present system, and he can scarcely repeat "devalue first and devalue most" (quoted by Peter Jay, *The Times*, 13.8.71), when all are compelled to revalue managed currencies (supposed to be floating) in order to save from collapse the American giant who so long had carried all their nonsense on his shoulders for the moderate commission of gradually possessing their economies. Here is a chance for Britain not to play small in trying to turn a quick penny between Europe and America with the slick trick of a currency independently managed until 1973, but to play great in the making of Europe and thus to regain lost time.

10

The Irish Problem

THE Irish problem is not simple, as anyone knows who has had experience of fighting and politics in that country. Yet there has been a solution for every question during my time in politics, often several and sometimes diverse solutions. What has generally been lacking is the will to act in time, and before long the Irish problem may require a high degree of will in British government.

My personal experience of Irish fighting was slight because I was on the Western front and then in hospital during the worst of the Irish wartime troubles, and was only sent to the Curragh after the '16 in a relatively quiet period. Later I was Parliamentary Secretary to the unofficial Bryce Commission to enquire into the conduct of the Black and Tans. In happier times I have twice lived in Ireland for short periods amid warm friendship of neighbours. Therefore it is possible to form a view of the present situation which is at least based on some practical experience.

The first necessity is to understand the nature of guerrilla war. The Irish are past masters of this operation, which baffled us in the Regular Army and later defeated the Black and Tans. What in reality do you do when you are moving through the countryside in proper military formation—point and flankers covering your advance—and your first man is shot as you enter a village? You fan out and rapidly envelop the village, moving at much greater speed than guerrillas because you are trained and equipped for mobile war and they are not. They are in the bag, and you comb the village only to find every woman knitting and every man digging the garden but no trace anywhere of a gun. What do you do next?—pull every house to pieces for evidence, or send for the Lord Chief Justice?

The Irish Problem

This was the first lesson in guerrilla war, and the world entirely failed to learn it. Guerrillas supported by a civilian population dedicated to the same cause can always baffle even the best Regular Army trained for full-scale war. Such an army cannot be used for indiscriminate terrorism designed to break the will of civilians supporting guerrillas, without discrediting its country in face of world opinion and destroying the morale of its own disciplined, honourable fighting men. Only an armed rabble can be used for such purposes and they are finally ineffective in face of experienced guerrillas. The Black and Tans contained both bad and good, but they were not comparable in training, discipline or morale to a Regular Army. They moved without any military precaution, driving around in open lorries and shooting indiscriminately to intimidate the local population; the only practical effect was to alert the next ambush just behind a high bank in a bend of the road which would slow them down. They lost in a few months far more killed than people would now tolerate in peace time, and this fact, in addition to our parliamentary opposition and American opinion, was enough for Lloyd George.

The present situation is even more difficult because it consists chiefly of urban guerrilla war, and it is still harder to locate the guerrilla if supported by the local population. The tactics of the professional soldiers now commanding in Ireland have been the best possible in these circumstances: mobile raids to discover arms by concentrated force which provides as little target as possible to snipers who fade into the civilian population after shooting. The contrary advice of Mr. Enoch Powell (19.2.71) was particularly inept, because it meant—if it meant anything—the permanent occupation of every trouble spot in Northern Irish cities. This would entail larger forces and the creation of military strong-points throughout the streets. The young soldier would thus present a permanent target to the well covered sniper and would be liable to stop a bullet directly he put his head above the parapet. Mobility and surprise in such fighting is preferable to the role of the sitting duck.*

Last Words : Broadsheets 1970-1980

British government in Northern Ireland should be moved by the right and natural desire of the British people to save the lives of their young soldiers as far as possible. I believe this objective can be combined with the best prospects for the interim task of maintaining order and for the ultimate political settlement of a united Ireland. The initial injustice of including a large Catholic population in Northern Ireland must now be corrected. The shelved report of the Boundaries Commission still exists; it was inadequate in doing justice to the Catholics but at least clarified boundary complexities sufficiently for determined action to transfer most of their population in the North to the South, taking a vote when possible. The task of the Army in keeping combatants apart until a settlement is reached would then be greatly simplified. The remaining Catholic areas in the North would be an inadequate base for effective guerrilla action, and reinforcement by infiltration from the South could be checked at the frontier. For the general purpose of the remaining operation the present Army should be used exclusively at the frontier, which could be held by lines of wire with intersecting block houses in a method long familiar to the British Army and now facilitated by helicopters and highly mobile ground weaponry. This would effectively close the frontier except for the main roads which can easily be controlled by check points. Mr. Powell's recent statement in Parliament (22.9.71) that Irish guerrillas depend on motorised transport again revealed the inadequacy of pedagogy; he could study with profit and possible sympathy the logistic capacities of the patient donkey.

The present very young soldiers should not be used against urban guerrillas, and above all British Government should not fall into the contrary and ultimately fatal error of permitting terrorist tactics by some new model of the Black and Tans. In the remaining interior of Ulster, a Defence Regiment properly weighted between Protestants and Catholics—and under proper control—should be able to keep order in these easier circumstances. If it cannot, a highly disciplined corps of war veterans and Army reservists should be recruited with good conditions for short time service; we need the experienced, and we can get them. Internment should end, not only because it again reduces Habeas Corpus to a squalid humbug, but also because a dozen of his relations and friends will feel in honour bound to take the place of every Irishman locked up. Our practical task is to hold the combatants apart in a military operation reduced to the feasible, and to treat each side with equal firmness and fairness. This solution is neither simple nor agreeable, but it is preferable to civil war. The very inconvenience of the arrangement may hasten the day when Irishmen of North and South come together within Europe. Frenchmen and Germans have done it already, and it is possible for Irishmen in regional arrangements which can lead to a true union of their country.

* Mr. Powell's advice appears the silliest thing said on such subjects since his remark (5.10.69) that the Channel was still an effective anti-tank ditch, meaning—if it meant anything—that a Russian army with the latest weapons, deployed along the Channel coast of a fallen Europe, would find it as difficult to get across as the Germans did in 1940. A man who believes that will believe anything, and will no doubt be unconvinced by the simple but conclusive statement of the government White Paper: "the Channel is no longer a barrier when the great powers are bridging space itself."

11

Speech to the Oxford Union

Supporting the motion "That this House would join the Common Market on the terms recommended by Her Majesty's Government."

BRITAIN'S ENTRY into Europe was one of those questions which must be regarded in the large. Our people must chiefly trust to their instincts because the subject was incapable of statistical proof either way. Rather than drown in a sea of conflicting figures they should keep their eyes fixed on the main facts. What actually happened when European peoples came together in an extensive living space of vast production and market potential? The answer was provided by the American standard of living. A wiser political system with the aid of modern technology could eventually multiply these benefits many times without incurring America's present disabilities.

Nevertheless, simple figures could sometimes throw light on the obscure but heated debate of those who claimed a Delphic authority as professional economists. For instance the main statistical point at issue between, the government White Paper and Mr. Wilson appeared to be the difference between £250,000,000 and £500,000,000 per annum in adverse effect on our balance of payments. Even if this charge were £500,000,000 a year, was that an overwhelming burden, an effective deterrent to a great people resolute to win a great future? Divide this £500,000,000 by the figure of our adult population, which is 37,000,000 over 19 years of age and we get £13.50 each per annum or 27 pence per week – the price of 20 cigarettes. What would history think of a people who turned away from destiny for the price of a packet of cigarettes? Surely even Mr. Wilson would find this charge supportable if translated into terms of pipe tobacco at least after writing his memoirs. The temporary charge imposed on our people by a decision affecting their whole future was at its worst, not very grave.

Mr. Jay might object that this method was too simplistic because it could be applied with almost equal effect to his still more exaggerated figures. Yet a reduction of expert subjects to simplicity was a necessary act of democratic politics, he sometimes contended that to simplify and synthesise were the chief arts of politics. In another example, it was generally claimed that progress belonged to the Left and order to the Right. Yet progress was impossible without order and order was finally impossible without progress. Synthesis of party differences at a higher level would eventually bring a national union which was at least temporarily essential to all great achievements. Such simple points could have some value, particularly in a period when Hegel was regarded as too complicated to be taught at Oxford University.

The real issue on Britain's entry into Europe was not any burden we might temporarily incur, which at the worst was trivial both in relation to the ultimate advantages and to the sacrifices our people had twice in his lifetime been asked to suffer in war-time Why was the supreme effort possible only for the destruction of war and never for the construction of peace which in this case was equally vital to our whole future? The real inhibition was the fear of any enlargement of life. It had no doubt arisen at each stage of progress, when we moved from the village fortress to the Anglo-Saxon kingdoms, and then further to the making of nations. When the first monkey dropped from the tree to the earth, or the first man moved from the cave to the sunlight, some old woman was whispering "be careful it is dangerous". Now Britain was told we would lose our sovereignty as we swung precariously between American defence and the economic control of international bankers.

Last Words : Broadsheets 1970-1980

The number of ways in which we have surrendered our sovereignty already has been repeated ad nauseam, and the real question was how to regain it in the equal partnership of a larger and stronger community.

A Brussels official had recently said with truth that the Common Market was not a finished building but a building site. Yet there was a fear that in joining with others for the building Britain must always get the worst of it. It was felt that in European discussion at a round table the Englishman must always be under it. That had not been his own experience. It was not long since England had been called perfide Albion because our diplomats looked so stupid and were so clever. Now there was an apprehension nurtured by Oxford intelligence that the French were much too smart both for our politicians and officials. Things do not change fundamentally in so short a time, and if this were the present case we should change our representative. A complex had been created by De Gaulle's veto, which in fact did not exist. Anyone who studied those Press conferences carefully would find that he said he would welcome Britain when the British became Europeans, but not before. Mr. Heath to his considerable credit had recently convinced Monsieur Pompidou that we were now Europeans, possibly with a little assistance from the background of German resurgence which he was no doubt too tactful to mention.

The Labour Party at their recent conference had done their best again to convince all Europe that the British people were not Europeans, with results that could be temporarily tragic if anyone took them seriously until a change of wind in the opinion polls swung them round again. What a spectacle Labour presented in face of the chance of the party's lifetime. The socialists were undoubtedly the strongest political force in present Europe, and all the parties who had long marched with Labour to the rousing music of the International were begging them to come in and speed the final victory. Once again Labour broke ranks and ran away. This was always their response to great opportunity, as it had been in 1931. They were then the government and had all the instruments of State in their hands when the long prophesied crisis of capitalism occurred. Then Labour promptly resigned. Was I wrong at that time to enquire in a Trafalgar Square meeting: "What must we think of a Salvation Army which takes to its heels on the Day of Judgement?"

Compassion was a great merit - probably the only remaining merit of the Labour Party and it moved them genuinely in the fear of any increase in food prices. Yet true compassion was effectively expressed in vigorously planning the future and working for the greatest good, of the greatest number, rather than in clinging to obsolete positions and grabbing anything going at the moment. The technological and market argument for European entry was overwhelming, and on this basis rested the material future. The proposed commitment was virtually limited to the material, and in accepting it our people need go no further unless they wished. Yet I believed that the very success of the eventual material achievement would later move them to larger aspirations. I had declared for the complete integration of Europe a Nation in 1948, not only because in this new and troubled age of science it would finally prove the only means of material survival but because three millennia of civilisation which had inspired the world must not again suffer the fate of disunion that had stricken its home of origin in classic Greece. European union using the genius of modern science could reach heights beyond even the furthest vision of the new generation.

12

Continental System Vs International Patchwork

ILLUSIONS die hard. We are now in the death throes of the hoary belief that international trade on a free market is the only way to run the world. All parties pay lip service to a system which dates from Adam Smith without noticing that facts have since changed. Yet the free market has conspicuously broken down in America, which was its outstanding example of success. A realistic President was obliged by the facts of life to reverse his policies almost overnight. Hence the tears and sweat of international coherences in efforts to re-patch a system which will break down again. Time presses for a real alternative.

America has long carried all the foibles and fallacies of the world on its shoulders. The central dilemma, that every country cannot at the same time sell more than it buys on world markets, was overcome by America running a trading deficit large enough to put all the others in artificial surplus, if their errors were less egregious than those of recent British governments. All could bask in the sunshine of a bogus paradise while the big boy carried the can, until the consequent inflation made it too hot to hold. Paper dollars to finance the deficit caused inflation in America as well as in the world at large, and enabled adroit financiers to use them for the purchase of other people's industries. The people suffered rising prices and industry suffered speculation; fun for the few while it lasted, but misery for the mass in the end. Serious statesmanship had to act.

For a moment it looked as if the action would be the building of a self-contained system in America; a practical possibility for a country of continental dimension, engaged in external trade only to about 4 per cent of its G.N.P. This caused consternation among Europeans, who have not yet dreamt that together they can be quite capable of doing the same. American realism faltered in face of foreign alarm, and the able Mr. Connally was despatched to bluff the partners and patch up the old roundabout. So far the process of repair simply means shifting the dilemma of the system from America to other shoulders less capable of bearing it. The arranged changes in currency parities will make it easier for America to sell goods and harder for others to sell them on world markets, but will make it no easier for all at the same time to sell more than they buy. The end of the American deficit can both acutely expose this fact and terminate the universal demand inflation. The euphoria of the U.S. world inflation was protracted because the American body largely absorbed the drug. But a private inflation by British government to replace it can operate more rapidly and more disastrously; from the latest figures it appears that the rate of increase in the money supply is much more than that of production. Inflation has never yet cured inflation, and finally a widespread loss of confidence can aggravate the unemployment which it is intended to prevent.

Hard facts teach quickly: it is now understood that cost inflation can still occur when demand inflation is checked. Direct action by government on wages and prices is recognised as necessary, and in America at least the negative aspects of a policy I first recommended in 1955 begin to be applied; even my own phrase "wage-price mechanism" is now used in place of the woolly "incomes policy" towards which British government was driven five years ago by facts, only to be repulsed by trade union pressure a few months later. The facts yet to be recognised are that the use of the wage-price mechanism should be positive as well as negative, and that any planned system of economics is incompatible with the free play of the world market. When government intervenes in an economic system either by the use of the wage-price mechanism to facilitate a true free enterprise, or to impose the restrictive controls of socialism cannot expose the process to the forces of global chaos. The elementary illusion that socialism could be created in one small island dependent for survival on international competition is now revealed by the abdication of the British Labour Party in favour of world capitalism.

Governments are now impelled by the logic of facts toward continental systems. America can only be lost if for too long it retreats into a patchwork of the old internationalism or fails to give effective and continuing economic leadership at home. Europe can only be saved if it makes a continental system with central authority adequate to give effective economic leadership. Otherwise we shall eventually revert to this tragic absurdity of all the relatively small European countries jockeying for the favoured position of an undervalued currency to support their exports, not only in competition with America but with one another, I warned against "competitive devaluation" years ago in Parliament. Where would America be today if each of its states behaved in this way? There is no answer to European problems except rapid integration. The reply of our local troglodytes "out of Europe, go it alone, float and make it dirtier still", would soon meet the inevitable fate of a nuisance island in partial or total exclusion from the markets of the developing continental systems.

What will happen to our "sovereignty" in a continental system? resounds the appeal of emotion, and what will happen in an insulated system to the profits earned by the City of London? echoes the appeal of the pocket. The answer is that the sovereignty will be greater and the profit will be increased. The City of London's particular expertise, ranging from a unique insurance system to the most diverse and ingenious operations of promotion, can offer a still wider service from a larger and stronger base. The European countries will be able to offer their particular expertise to the world with more effect from the continental system, and will be more appreciated when they withdraw in favour of an enlarged home market from cut-throat competition in manufactured goods which the whole Western world and much of the East are now equally capable of producing.

Continental System Vs International Patchwork

Sovereignty will be greater the more complete the integration, and influence within that sovereignty will be available to those who can persuade, exactly as it is today within our national communities. Three-tier government - European, national and regional will protect the various cultures of our peoples by central strength now lacking, and enhance them by the diversification which further devolution will promote. If we can make Europe, the world will follow: others will save themselves by creating similar systems. Europe and America can and should devote a proportion of their wealth to enabling this to happen in the third world, just as individuals of goodwill help others in private life. European relations with America wall steadily improve when we are off their hands and off their markets, true to our alliance when danger threatens either, but as a colleague rather than a satellite.

These policies which appear "way out" today, will become practical when the failure of the present system is finally recognised; "sharp is the glance of necessity". We have already seen policies reversed overnight when need arose. Clear ideas and firm action must be ready when need is greater.

13

Stop this Anarchy - Maintain the Law

THE abdication of government during the recent preliminary crisis is now proved in two respects. It handed over the economic life of the nation to an outside body, It delegated the maintenance of law and order to the variable discretion of local constables, Mr. Carr said on television that whatever the decision of the Wilberforce Tribunal the government would accept it. A body elected by no-one was promoted from an advisory capacity to be the arbiter of our economic destiny and the master of a defeated government. Mr. Maudling stated that "anything beyond peaceful picketing is illegal... If there is danger to life and limb, it arises from illegal picketing". (*The Times* 10.2.72). Ample evidence was provided, even by other ministers, that much picketing was illegal. Yet Mr. Maudling added: "It is not for the Government to order Chief Constables". The abdication both in economic decision and in maintenance of law at that point became complete. Whether this attitude is novel or traditional, it is evident that in a time of crisis government was not in the picture. It remains to draw a lesson for the future from events only too likely to recur.

Government undoubtedly had ample powers under existing law to deal with the situation. An effective parliament might well enquire what is the use of granting further powers to governments which shrink from using those they possess already? Admittedly, the strange timidity in dealing with flagrant illegality was partly due to their surprise at the strength of public support for the miners' "special case". But this in turn was due to government failure to foresee events, and to their flicker of mistaken resolution in refusing to intervene in "market forces", apart from a wooden, rule-of-thumb negative applied exclusively to the nationalised industries. The conscious and deliberate use of the wage-price mechanism, which I have advocated since 1955, would have prevented this situation arising, by elected government implementing our people's sense of social justice. The less defined equivalent of an "incomes policy", to which public opinion is now moving slowly but inexorably, is inadequate if purely negative, and recent events illustrate this fact.

There is a "special case" in the national and human interest for such categories as miners and dustmen in particularly arduous or disagreeable occupations at one end of the scale and, at the other, for scientists, highly skilled technicians, doctors, nurses, etc., who lack the massive support of the big battalions, but who should be the special charge of a government elected by the whole people to secure the country's well-being. We should surmount such absurdities as the contention of Mr. Russell Lewis of the Conservative Political Centre in defending market forces, that it is right for a pop singer to receive ten times 'the salary of a cabinet minister because "the pop singer can fill the Albert Hall", while "for a cabinet minister, the audience would have to be press ganged". Having often experienced no difficulty in filling the Albert Hall or even the Earl's Court Exhibition Hall which holds several times as many, I still do not feel that on this account alone I should receive ten times as much as a cabinet minister, and I surmise that in this respect at least the majority of my fellow countrymen would agree with me.

Government in the modern world must give an economic lead, or in effect, cease to govern. This does not mean the universal controls of obsolete socialism, still less of communism. It means a consciously dirigiste government determining the main lines of reward differentials through appropriate instruments in constant consultation with the trade unions. It means also that government should be supplied with a general staff which continuously strives to foresee events and to avoid surprise in a shifting and menacing situation, just as the general staff of an army, by contingency planning in peace, averts shock and prepares to seize opportunity when need arises. In short, we need something like the comprehensive organisation I suggested long ago in resignation from the government, rather than the recent appointment of one estimable scientist and a few assistants preoccupied with the equally important but less urgent problems of pure research.

There remains the paramount question of maintaining the law with sufficient means. No sympathy with the miners should blind us to this need. Personally, I have retained such sympathy ever since the days when they elected me, from the political side, to address their annual galas at Durham and elsewhere, while from the trade union side they elected my friend, the miners' leader A. J. Cook, whose vibrant personality would reduce present revolutionaries to pale shadows. Yet sentiment must not obscure the experience that the violent and entirely illegal prevention of other people's lawful business defeated an unprepared government, though apparently the usual external elements rather than the miners were chiefly responsible.

The gravity of these events is enhanced by the vagaries of present welfare benefits seeming indirectly to have subsidised the transport of "pickets" in open paramilitary operations. Above all, we face the outstanding fact that once a government is on the run, this is likely to happen again.

I have long suggested a national police force not to supersede local constabularies, but to take over if and when they prove inadequate. Otherwise the ultimate resort is the army, and history sadly recalls Featherstone, where Mr. Asquith assumed responsibility for opening fire on miners. A national police force can avert such bitter decisions. Also, in contingency of considerable disorder, political or industrial, it would free the local police forces for their proper and hardly diminishing business of preventing' ordinary crime. Modern science can provide the new force with a wide variety of disagreeable though harmless means to control riot, but forethought, planning, equipment and training are needed. A national police force is the answer, and time presses beyond the decision or will of present politicians.

It is indeed a sombre national scene, illumined only by the pathetic little jokes of Mr. Wilson, received with the rapturous inanity of his admirers, while disorder in parliament reflects disorder in the country. His reference to Nero's "heating system" was inadvertently quite apt for the inflated leader of an inflationist party. Party decadence can only confront national tragedy with a giggle or a scuffle. The steady dedication of Mr. Heath to the beginning of Europe shines by contrast. It is the best hope of Britain until an awakened resolution can summon to government the whole vitality of the country in a situation as serious as war.

Meantime, Britain's European destiny may possibly be postponed but not finally frustrated by the incongruous alliance of the conspicuously disinterested Mr. Foot with an ambitious pedant who first came to popular notice at the age of fifty-six with a belated but hysterical speech on coloured immigration, after polling under five per cent of the votes in a previous bid for party leadership. If the patchwork coalition of little Englanders succeed in temporarily dividing our country, now bereft of Commonwealth, from its only opportunity of renewed greatness in Europe, Mr. Powell would be an appropriate though transient Prime Minister for the offshore island to which their negations would reduce Great Britain.

14

Free Speech and New Ideas

America - Europe - Continental Systems

SHOULD any alternative to the present system be discussed? I have recently had the chance to do this in America in 29 interviews reported to be "aired" over 474 separate television stations and 2,432 radio stations, coast to coast. Why cannot we have similar discussion within our available means in Britain? Is it desirable that we should? Or is it really better and safer just to go on debating small variations in the same ideas among the same people, until some explosion bewilders them all and rocks the State? In America we usually agreed to divide the discussion 50/50 between past and present, which chiefly concerned the recent breakdown of the Bretton Woods system of international trade. The basic problem is that each country cannot at the same time sell more than it buys. Any child in a first year maths class could see this, but our political and economic pundits spend interminable international conferences beating their heads against this fact. To draw attention to it is not to become a "terrible simplificateur", but to insist that we should see the whole wood as well as the jungle of ancient trees and scrub undergrowth of recent detail, in which experts often get lost.

How then is it that this system worked with only temporary interruptions, ever since the war, and has succeeded in producing the affluent society, albeit at the cost of continually rising prices which threaten to develop into the worst of all crashes—inflation? The answer is that America has been content to carry the western world on its shoulders by running an enormous trading deficit. Stripped of jargon, this deficit was made good by paper dollars which put everyone else in artificial surplus most of the time. But the inevitable result was the start of a major inflation at home which President Nixon began to check only just in time. Measures were taken to curb the expansion of the deficit, and Mr. Connally was despatched to put to America's trading partners the shocking suggestion that they should share the burden of this failing system. The outcome was exchange adjustments which will make it easier for America to sell goods on world markets and harder for the rest of us, but will not make it possible for all simultaneously to sell more than they buy.

The idea I suggested was that continental systems should replace the international system of Bretton Woods. They must be viable areas, containing most of their own raw materials. With the aid of modern science they could each possess a productive potential exceeding that of the whole world a few decades ago. They would exchange specialities but would not engage in cut-throat competition of manufactured goods which nowadays can be equally well produced almost anywhere on the globe. Consequently each government of such an area, and the people who elect it, would become completely the masters of their own economic fate instead of the presently helpless victims of "external factors". Is it not evident in the light of experience that only in this way can a planned economy operate, whether it be the guided American capitalism, socialism, communism, or a new idea in united Europe? The free play of world market forces is now seen again simply to bring world chaos; these forces are only regulated, if at all, by international combines and cartels, by finance and trade union power.

Certain advantages of a relatively self-contained area under its own economic authority are clear. For example, a proper balance between growth and ecology can then be maintained. A firm operating within the international system has a simple reply when told to stop pollution: this costs money and raises our production costs; consequently we shall be priced out of foreign markets. Only a government free from the world costing system can hold a proper balance between growth, amenity and leisure.

Last Words : Broadsheets 1970-1980

Similarly it could check the constant rise in prices caused by the demand inflation of an excessive money supply which is designed to preserve industrial peace and prevent disruption of the export trade, but in the end aggravates industrial strife. Any consequent unemployment could be overcome by constructive works which would add much to good living within an area insulated from external costing and chaotic competition. The present cost-push inflation, accentuating the demand inflation through the overweening power of organised sectional interests, could also be more readily met by a government unafraid of bankruptcy on its balance of payments. Trade in manufactured goods could be entirely internal in a region of continental dimension.

The massive question of natural economic and political divisions would of course require a considerable effort of international negotiation. North and South America, Europe. Africa, Russia, China and finally Japan and India are primarily indicated. The intermediate areas between them and the inter-relationship of the countries within them also demand careful thought and debate: clear answers are usually available if there is a will to find a way. The complete political integration I favour for Europe would render organisation more effective, but common economic arrangements are yet compatible with the jealously guarded national sovereignties to which others still adhere. What matters first is a rational division of the world into economic spheres which are free from mutually destructive competition, and are thus competent to develop their diverse civilisations without outside interference. A competitive but more genuinely peaceful co-existence could then develop between American capitalism, two varieties of communism in Russia and China, and new ideas within a united Europe.

The future of the world might eventually be settled not by theory but by the proved fact of the most successful system. Forcible interference with each other can be prevented by maintaining the nuclear balance unless and until a reciprocal disarmament can be agreed. The present attempts of communism to intervene politically within other countries could be met by a very active retaliation in the battle of ideas with all the means of propaganda which technology can now provide, or could be ignored in the calm assurance that the success of our freer economic system would become so evident that disruptive efforts would prove derisory against any government strong enough to maintain internal order and external defence.

These ideals may be regarded as futuristic or way out, but are they not worth discussing while there is still time? It would have been better to debate the question of national sovereignty when I first said "Europe a Nation" in 1948 than to begin thinking about it when we are at the end of the European queue in 1972. Better to have discussed an incomes policy in 1955 when I began to develop the "wage-price mechanism"; a phrase recently repeated by *Time* magazine in America, 18.10.71, while reviewing the President's new policies. Why is it possible to discuss anything within the bounds of reason in America and nothing outside the narrowing circle of contemporary banality in Britain? One answer given to me was that 60 competitive radio stations exist in the New York district alone, all eager for news and novel ideas, making much nonsense but also some sense.

The concept of a broadcasting trust really dedicated to the service of truth and complete intellectual freedom is of course finer. Nothing could be better than an entirely disinterested order of service eliciting the facts of the present and seeking the truth of the future. Failing this, the diversity of America is preferable, although they make enormous mistakes. For instance, they invented the youth cult, which landed them with Kennedy and thus with the Vietnam war. The Germans once fell into a very different variety of the same error, but then turned to Adenauer who retired aged 88 after the "economic miracle". Yet free discussion can produce things more important than mistakes - creative achievements which are born of new ideas.

15

When the Nonsense Has to Stop

Another Fall of the Pound

NOW the nonsense has to stop: a real government would ask the British people to say this at a General Election. There is a plain word for the nonsense —decadence. Every serious person knows it, but most hesitate to say it. Yet I firmly believe that all this is mostly froth on the surface. Beneath it the great river of national life flows on, the vital stream of thinkers, men of action, scientists, technicians and skilled workers who once led the world and could again.

The problem is how to free our nation from the smother of contemporary decadence: the powerless State and the all-powerful interests; inflation with all its consequence; money for all except the deserving who are crushed by taxation; the heaven of spivs and speculators, the hell of the old beset by rising prices and of the young seeking a decent home; crime and violence rampant in the face of blinking authority which refuses a national police force; the shrill giggle of flaunting vice, silly or sadistic, doping and debauching British children, mocking our country to the world. Enough of this catalogue to which more could be added. We know it; the question is what to do? I will be precise, and the reader can judge.

First we need a union of men and women drawn from every vital source in the nation and adequate to win the confidence of the country. This means the best of politics, business, trade unions, civil service, universities and the defence services. Some now say, and write, the fighting forces alone. As a professional soldier in the first war, and also as a child of parliament which made my reputation, I take a different view. The realistic, military attitude is a valuable ingredient in a government of action, but cannot be the whole. Britain is not a banana republic, and the British would never sit on bayonets. We can still do things in our own way.

This union of the entire nation should ask the people for a majority at a normal General Election. An enabling bill should then be passed giving government sufficient power of action, subject to the right of parliament to dismiss it at any time by vote of censure. M.P.s should spend most of their time among their constituents to tell the people what government is doing and to tell the government what people are thinking. They should also retain the right to interrogate ministers at regular intervals, and, in a new procedure, a committee of M.P.s from all parties should be attached to each department the better to inform themselves of government working.

Such a government should frequently meet the people face to face on television and at press conferences. Similar facilities should be available to opposition parties. Freedom of speech would always be carefully preserved by anyone unafraid of debate. No party, or parties, responsible for the present situation could thus unite the country, because the people would ask: "why have you not done this already"? Yet within the old parties are many splendid people who would selflessly contribute to the national effort as they did in wartime. The proposed action would be a temporary effort, as in wartime—the purpose to clean up Britain. After the normal life of parliament the old ways could return if the people so desired, or they could decide for a modernised parliamentary system after full argument by all parties at another election. What now matters is that during a period of national union the necessary action should be taken.

We could stop inflation and stabilise prices. If the end of an excess money supply brought temporary unemployment, it could be solved by constructive works of permanent national value. The principle that elected government rather than sectional interests should determine the main lines of reward would be fearlessly upheld in a real incomes policy, and prices would equally be controlled whenever necessary.

The land racket would be smashed, and houses would be built by mass-production in a national effort as an operation of war. Recent immigrants would queue up to return if we actively assisted their homelands to mutual benefit. These are just a few, brief and necessarily crude illustrations of what could be done by a government of action. Would such a government make mistakes? Yes, of course, no men are infallible, but it should have the manhood to admit errors to the people, and to learn from them. We need a renaissance of manhood. Possibly ideas such as these may prompt the renewal of recent writing about "Mosley waiting for the call". In fact, I prefer to do television in four languages, and to publish articles, urging closer European union and thus assisting world peace; recently I have been able to begin this contribution, while remaining always in close touch with people and events in Britain. But obviously, like other Englishmen, I am ready with my compatriots wherever they may be, if wanted, to serve our country.

The fall of the pound is due to two basic reasons often noted in these columns. 1, Inflation never yet cured inflation. 2, All nations cannot simultaneously sell more than they buy, and one or other is therefore always in trouble under the present international system. The causes of the inflation are an increase of over 20 per cent in the money supply during twelve months, and an average increase in wage settlements of at least double the best hope of the government for increased production without counting the new pace in inflation set by the mining and railway awards. This combination of demand - pull inflation through an excess money supply with the cost - push inflation of such wage settlements made sooner or later inevitable the present de facto devaluation.

Yet during this process the government agreed a settlement in Washington last December which made easier the sale of

When the Nonsense Has to Stop

American goods on world markets and harder the sale of British exports. To crown this record of folly Mr. Barber then intimated to the world that he was ready to devalue the pound rather than to check the inflation, and Mr. Healey announced that devaluation was imminent. In short, the parties have muddled and chattered the pound away, and now risk to muddle and chatter away our whole European position.

In this stampede British government has not only torn up the Washington agreement which President Nixon described as "the most significant monetary agreement in the history of the world", but has also scrapped Britain's signature this Spring to the agreement that members of the European community would hold their currency values within 2.25 per cent of each other s value. The object is blatantly to make our exports more competitive against our fellow-members of the E.E.C. and against America, not by checking inflation and putting our house in order, but by playing financial tricks which we have just promised to eliminate from the system. In short, our government joined the club with a solemn pledge to obey its rules and within two months began again to play the old card trick on fellow-members. Can we be surprised if governments of our old parties become less welcome guests in Europe, when the suspicions of the late General de Gaulle are so speedily and amply confirmed?

And what good does it all do to Britain? A floating exchange rate is an effective, temporary device for an isolated and embattled island. I recommended it myself in the Birmingham Proposals of 1925, and it is just that much out of date. All the others have now rumbled the trick and can do the same when it suits them; then we are back to square one. Further, since those days the continental systems have begun to form, and, if we make ourselves nuisance enough for long enough with slick financial tricks we risk final exclusion from both the European and American markets. There is really no alternative in modern conditions to putting our own house in order and becoming a good colleague in the new Europe. This means stopping our inflation and facing the consequences from which present governments shrink, by meeting the temporary un-employment with dynamic policies. This requires in turn an altogether different order of mind and will in a government given the mandate to act by vote of the people at a General Election. Then we can begin the task of replacing the international breakdown by agreement on rational and viable continental systems.

16

Notes on the Situation

HAS Britain undertaken in Ulster a police operation conducted by the Army, or a military exercise, an operation of war? The question is vital both in terms of present efficiency and of the ultimate peace settlement. It now appears to be treated as a police job, but young soldiers face skilful sniping, and lethal booby traps set by experts with a long tradition of guerrilla fighting, protected by a civilian population in Catholic areas mostly dedicated to what they passionately believe is their country's cause. The result is a pitiful loss of young lives and a continuing anarchy which mocks British rule. A military operation is exactly the opposite method, which I suggested a year ago; the complete closure of a shortened and tenable frontier, based on the original boundary commission findings which remitted the bulk of the Catholic population to the south.

It is idle to argue that closing the frontier by two lines of wire intersected by blockhouses is impossible, because the British Army did it in South Africa at the turn of the century over a larger area; since those days they have the additional means of aircraft, helicopters and armoured vehicles to patrol the lines, and the possibility of many new scientific devices between them. The flaccid objection that the I.R.A. will then circumvent the closure by sea can be overcome by the same fast motor boats used in the Channel during the last war, or by mining appropriate waters with due notice, which could also be given to airplanes liable to fire if they crossed the frontier without permission. The present infiltration of guerrillas and weapons from the south could thus be completely stopped, and that essential means of protracted warfare — periodic withdrawal of front line troops for rest — could also be denied to them. The military operation could then be made entirely effective, and a genuinely impartial police force could maintain order in Belfast between the Protestant majority and the remaining Catholic minority, members of which should be offered transfer to the south on generous terms if they wished.

This is not in itself a settlement but a decisive step toward it. Directly we face the fact of a war situation we eliminate the confusion which now inhibits possibility of peace. You can only end a war with a lasting peace by dealing at some point with the men who are doing the fighting. To be baffled in an ineffective police operation and then to declare that you will never meet the I.R.A. and will continue indefinitely to answer "ferocity with ferocity", is to get the worst of all worlds: no peace, scant prospect of enduring military success, some discredit of the British name if words are implemented which are inappropriate to soldier or statesman.

We have lived through all this before, but our politicians never learn. Michael Collins was nominated "chief of the murder gang" and the "hunted fugitive" was to be shot on sight. A few weeks after such utterances he was seated in Downing Street exchanging jokes and amenities with Lloyd George, Churchill and F. E. Smith. He was the man who had led the fighting and he stood true to his word when he made the peace at the cost of his own life. A promise implicit in the settlement was never honoured: the inclusion in the south of most of the Catholic population of Ulster after the report of the boundary commission. Is such a peace now impossible because passions are more inflamed? Feeling ran high before, when fourteen of our officers were shot in their beds during the night by young men who had spent the previous evening praying in a chapel. It was atrocious, but peace had to come in the end. The very inconvenience of a closed frontier could promote peace because it will inevitably induce joint counsel between north and south gradually to make possible normal life again, and this in turn can lead to joint council as both enter Europe with all its possibilities of a better life.

Notes on the Situation

The agreed union of Ireland with European safeguards for all minority regions is in the end inevitable and can thus be expedited. The sad belief of a growing number of British people that justice serves only the interest, convenience or prejudices of those in power will not be diminished by the differential treatment of the I.R.A. and U.D.A. The Times reported (19.8.72): "The Government is known to be seriously concerned at the threat that the Ulster Defence Association made last night to kill provisional I.R.A. members who fall into their hands, although it is difficult to see what action could be taken. Even if the leaders of U.D.A. were arrested the violence that might follow would outweigh the advantage of convicting a few men. All day uniformed members of the U.D,A., who are to march at a rally in Belfast tomorrow, were checking cars entering or leaving loyalist areas. They set up "obstructions", etc., interesting information to the original objects of the Public Order Act, who wore uniform simply and successfully to defend free speech at their own meetings when government proved incapable of maintaining order, and a searchlight on present impartiality of government in preventing murder in Ulster.

Dock Lessons, Planning Staff, National Police

THE latitude given to militant and sometimes armed dockers to travel about the country with the aid of public funds (supplementary benefits) and to assault the police, will also not enhance regard for government's resolution in maintaining law. Two larger lessons emerge from this dismal experience. (1) The dockers had a real grievance which could be foreseen. Similar cases will presently arise in the age of automation and computers. Workers in dying industries must be phased out with retraining and redeployment. Government more than ever requires a planning staff which I have recommended ever since resignation in 1930. This idea is now again being discussed in a too comprehensive and consequently amorphous and confused form. We need a relatively few experts drawn from the whole diversity of the nation with nothing to do but look ahead; a small, closely knit staff to serve a Prime Minister's initiative and inspiration through all existing departments. America has now made a start with some forethought; must we always lag? (2) The national police force I have also urged is now being proved necessary. Present police forces should use traditional methods until the situation gets beyond them. Then the nonsense has to stop, and a force must enter with all modern devices of non-lethal riot control, otherwise when the police have failed, the military is called in, with the possibility of tragedy, as happened in the Featherstone troubles when Asquith was Home Secretary. The situation can be very serious in a modern economic crisis.

Asian Immigrants

I APOLOGISE for so much "I told you so"; always a graceless and unpopular situation. Yet it is essential to show that myopic lack of foresight, coupled with a traditional but obsolete vanity, can lead our country to recurrent troubles. The time to deal with immigration was in 1959, when I stood at the General Election inter alia on a demand to stop it; there were then only 300,000 immigrants in Britain. We met with a storm of abuse, and a Conservative M.P., who ventured near the same position, was called a moral leper by a recent Prime Minister. Subsequently all parties were obliged to agree to restrictive measures, and a minister of 1962, engaged at least in collective Cabinet responsibility for the introduction of immigrants and hand-out of passports, now assumes the freedom to attack his colleagues for the results, with considerable improvement of his political position but without benefit to a country plunged into this situation; hysterical language without constructive remedy is the last thing required. Must leadership always be from behind? We need a change in the whole mind and character of government before worse occurs than the Ugandan ignominy, where there is not even a whisper of Rhodesian sanctions. Determined but also creative action is again required on a scale beyond the compass of present politics.

Notes on the Situation

Inflation

WE come to the end of "a year in which the money supply has been rising at a rate of nearly 30 per cent" (*Financial Times*, 17 and 24.8.72), while "during the last year, money has grown at a 5.3 per cent annual rate" in America (*New York Herald Tribune*, 2.9.72). Britain approaches with gathering momentum a runaway inflation, and at this point experience is a better guide than theory. Will anything be done to stop it? *The Times* reported (17.7.72) Mr. Patrick Jenkin, Chief Secretary of the Treasury, as saying: "A restriction of the money supply would check economic growth. It is politically unacceptable".

It is true that the end of inflation can bring a temporary unemployment, but this can be overcome by energetic measures of government to move the economy forward again on a stable price level. Yet present government shrinks from the "politically unacceptable", because it cannot persuade people that action is necessary. Once again we require a change of mind and character in a government which dares to give a clear lead and tell the nation in plain language what needs to be done. Government is responsible for the general demand inflation caused by an excess money supply under its own control, and trade unions in an uncontrolled monopoly position are responsible for the particular cost inflation of wage demands far exceeding any immediate prospect of increased production; "earnings 12 per cent above those of a year ago" (*Financial Times*, 26.8.72) and predicted now to rise by 15 per cent per annum (*National Institute*, 31.8.72). This combination is the basic cause of the continually rising prices which afflict our people at every turn of their daily lives and may soon threaten the life of the country. The facts are clear: the remedies have long been defined, and in America are now partly implemented with a large measure of success. We need government with the nerve and will to act.

17

European Achievement Vs Nonsense Policies

FORTUNATE is the statesman to whom falls the honour of taking Britain into Europe. Mr. Heath has well earned this high distinction with much skill and pertinacity in face of malicious attacks and nonsense policies. Cheers are due even from the ranks of Tuscany — who believe that only a government drawn from the whole nation can meet the coming crisis, whose gravity has just been emphasised from Cambridge. Yet the country appears from opinion polls still to be almost evenly divided on the question of European entry, and it may therefore be of some service to examine the alternative. What does the odd coalition of negation really propose? The answer can only be an offshore island going it alone. By what means, we may enquire?

Mr. Powell's only clear reply has been a floating exchange rate. Quite a good suggestion in an emergency, which the Government has since adopted. Better still in the Birmingham Proposals of 1926, before everyone became acutely aware of the artificial advantage temporarily given to export trade by devaluations which now threaten to become competitive. But can anyone imagine that financial tricks to undercut them on their own markets will long be permitted to an outside power by the continental economies? It was quite a strain when Britain recently scrapped the agreements reached on exchange parities in Rome last March and in Washington the previous December, This was tolerated temporarily as the price of easing our European entry; a considerable concession in the light of the French President's last Press conference. What hope would there be for us permanently playing the banana republic on European and American markets with successive devaluations engineered by dirty flotations. The end must be total exclusion from markets on which Britain depends to sell the bulk of our foreign trade, and the same measure could defeat other devious substitutes for the arduous task of putting our own house in order. How then would Mr. Powell's free market—the free-for-all of the 19th century—operate in face of closed continental systems and international cartels, strongly based within those systems for more effective competition on remaining markets?

Where else can our country turn? Could the Dominions take the place of Europe and America, or have President Amin and his friends either the desire or the means to kiss the other cheek if we turn it often enough? These are nonsense policies. Canadian industries under American control are not going to provide an alternative market, even if it were adequate. Australia and New Zealand are unlikely to risk their dependence on American alliance and military support to bolster the stop-go economy of an intermittently bankrupt island on the other side of the globe, just for old times sentiment. The only hope of ever restoring that happy and fruitful relationship is to use the powerful magnet of a developed European economy. Japan, America and communism confront our export trade in the Far East. Even the international expertise of the City of London would find it harder to operate without than within a continental system. In short, the economic alternative to European entry does not exist for Britain. The combined opposition's economic notions are as grotesque as Mr, Powell's dictum in the military sphere that the Channel is still an effective anti-tank ditch: well met by the Government White Paper's succinct rejoinder that no longer presented an obstacle to powers now capable of bridging space itself. In every sphere the negative rests quite simply on nonsense policies, which are only worth considering because the coalition of negation is still supported by half the country.

All the consistent ability and personal integrity of Mr. Foot cannot mask the inherent absurdity of his position on the other trapeze of the chaotic circus. To discover Mr. Wilson's exact position on the roundabout at any given moment would tax the skill and patience of the most experienced ringmaster. The Labour Party like all systems in decline produces its own caricature. There was always a strange paradox in the belief that socialism could be created in one small island entirely dependent for its economic life on the world markets of the capitalist system. This little difficulty finally impelled our local socialists to recognise the Empire they had so long detested, just as their policies brought it to an end. The rousing strains of the Internationale had long inspired them to embrace the world; yet when the comradely arms of Herr Brandt and all their nearest socialist neighbours were wide open to receive them, they promptly turned round and fled. Nothing is so terrifying to the Labour Party as the prospect of any real achievement. This performance baffles the satirists, they cannot gild the lily. My old enquiry.......what are we to think of a Salvation Army which takes to its heels on the day of judgement? - becomes jejune, pallid beside this last, full-blooded comedy. Where now is the Second Internationale? Where the world of brotherhood? In the hushed silence of international socialism it was left to Mr. Powell occasionally to sally from behind his anti-tank ditch for addresses to the dark regions beyond Calais. Meaning to describe himself as an ex-member of the Shadow Cabinet he referred to the "ombre cabinet", and evoked from Frenchmen the sympathy due to any unfortunate who finds himself in a lavatory when the lights go out. The foreign policies of the motley coalition remain as obscure as their prospects of economic survival.

Yet despite every absurdity the negation remains fortified by the opinion polls in combination with Mr. Heath's electoral reference to the whole-hearted support of the people; a minor delinquency in comparison with many utterances on such occasions. Demand for a referendum was made in the name of the Constitution. Yet again fact was stood on its head, because referendum does not exist in the Constitution. Personally, I have always been in favour of the referendum in principle, but to embody it in the Constitution would require an election on that issue and the approval of the people. At present this demand is the exact reverse of the constitutional position. The question of European entry, on the other hand, has been before the country for over a decade. If, any elector failed to question his candidate on that subject at the last Election it was his own fault. The present constitutional position is that Parliament decides, and Parliament has decided. The rest is confused crying of cats on a wintry roof.

The recently expressed desire for Britain to be "bloody-minded" within the Community formulates the pious hope of some politicians to become as big a nuisance to the Europeans as they have been to their fellow-countrymen. The impractical policy of renegotiation ignores the live possibility of continual and constructive negotiation in the organic development of Europe. A Brussels official recently remarked that only the basement of the Community so far existed, while the whole building awaited construction. The influence of Britain in that task will depend on the voices which represent it, on the weight of our economy and the dynamism of our ideas. To implement our policies within a democracy we have to persuade other people to accept them. That process in simple principle is transferred to a larger sphere, but the democratic process remains the same.

This confused thinking about sovereignty rests on the bizarre concept that Messrs. Heath, Wilson and Thorpe will sit for ever in a solid block icily confronting the equally monolithic block of Messrs. Pompidou and Mitterand, while some conspiracy of foreigners places our whole nation in a permanent minority. Muddle of mind is matched by ignorance of the European situation. Yet happily the fog begins to lift with some serious discussion in the British Press, following a political fanfare of entry so dull that Bernard Shaw would have again described it as "the funeral march of a fried eel". Where is the enthusiasm of a great campaign to reveal the real choice between reversion to an isolated, beleaguered island, and rapid advance to a complete European democracy with its own institutions and new political alignments? They will be based on the ideas of a scientific age

Last Words : Broadsheets 1970-1980

which will surmount atavistic prejudice in a larger patriotism, and in strength of union will preserve, and even enhance, the brightly varied strands of justly cherished national cultures. The debate of the future awaits the British people.

18

Britain in Danger - The Need for Real Change

IN the year 1980 the French standard of life will be double that of the British. The French Finance Minister was recently able to make this statement with the support of impartial American statistics. The question is whether the British people will allow this trend to continue, or possibly worse? What has happened?— Why this sharp reversal of fortune? The only apparent answer is that for a period the French had a different kind of government. It remained entirely democratic, and both leadership and party were ready to yield to the popular vote. Mistakes were made, but the psychology of the country was changed and a renaissance occurred. Are we capable in a British way of a similar achievement, and possibly much more?

What are the essentials of effective action in the present situation? The first is a new parliamentary majority drawn from the whole nation, which could either be attained with one or more of the existing party machines, or possibly with an improvised machine; method is a matter of detail, though important. The second is an Emergency Powers Act which would allow government to act more rapidly in continually changing circumstances, subject always to the right of Parliament to dismiss it at any time by vote of censure; that is vital. What then should we do? Reply should be made with the full awareness that experience brings: information supplied by the main departments alters many preconceptions, and has hitherto rendered party programmes mostly bogus. Yet, in office, mind and will in combination can always find more than one answer to the problems facing government.

Last Words : Broadsheets 1970-1980

The first task is to overcome inflation. This requires the double action of limiting the presently inflated money supply to the potential of production and of curbing monopoly power with a policy for wages and prices. The former without the latter would create massive unemployment and bankrupt many small businesses before key trade unions and dominant finance yielded to the national interest. Their uncontrolled monopoly power would still enable them to obtain an even more disproportionate share of the limited money supply, unless and until the main body of industry was prostrated by deflation. Reasonable limitation means an end to the present reckless overspending by government in a public sector it should never have entered: the support of lame ducks hobbling under a failing private enterprise; the subsidy of nationalised industries instead of confronting them with economic management or radical change; the payment of industrial Danegeld whenever trouble looms. This passive reaction makes government the victim rather than the master of events. All stems from the root error that rulers can inflate out of difficulty; a mistake as old as history. Inflation of the weak seventies can prove even more disastrous than the deflation of the tough twenties.

Ending inflation will cause unemployment which will not cure itself; experience exposes this basic fallacy of the simple monetarists. Further action will the be needed to move the economy forward again on a stable price level and government for this purpose should gradually enter a different public sector which is its legitimate and necessary sphere: creative works which are too big for private enterprise, such as rehousing the people as an operation of war, dealing with pollution, the long overdue clean up of Britain, support of science adequate to secure the future. Temporary adversity suffered after the inflation could be turned to high advantage by a determined government supported by a people who responded to an appeal for great action.

Our people in recent years have been fed with too many illusions. It is another deception to say that we can come through this trouble

Britain in Danger - The Need for Real Change

without effort and sacrifice. If we drift to deeper danger a wartime or siege economy may be a temporary necessity. Then objectives must be clearly defined and firmly held, while sacrifice must be really equal and speculative profiteering ruthlessly eliminated. Some economic leadership of government will always be necessary even in a normal period, now that the 19th century free market has changed to monopoly power both national and multi-national. Government must obtain fair reward for those who cannot protect themselves, whether skilled scientists and others vital to the nation's well-being, or the unorganised and helpless. If it secures fair wages in constant consultation with trade unions throughout genuinely competitive industry, profits are automatically and justly determined, the efficient making much, and the inefficient little. When true incentives thus exist, funds for investment will be available for the successful and expanding in an assured and stable market. It will only be necessary to control prices in the case of monopolies; otherwise competition will keep prices down. These things are possible, but the confusion of present thinking requires further and clearer discussion.

The greater a viable economic area, the greater the economic freedom. Europe with no internal balance of payments problems could clearly be freer than an island subject to stop-go; such questions should no more exist within our continent than between Yorkshire and Lancashire. Having taken the decision to enter Europe, plain sense is to press on and make a job of it. But we have first to put our own house in order, to reap the benefit of European entry. Even the first effective common action is now frustrated because the pound is too weak for safety in a joint flotation against the dollar. Co-operation on condition of being kept for ever is an embarrassing marriage contract. Yet we cannot live longer with successive devaluations disguised as flotations, because we dare not take action to become truly competitive. To join the Community effectively, and work together, we must quickly be restored to health and strength. The present government has earned the supreme merit of taking us into Europe, but after abdication in favour of Wilberforce it

Last Words : Broadsheets 1970-1980

became doubtful if it could do much more. The task will require a concentration of the whole nation as in time of war, and a sequent spirit of renaissance.

Let no men of value be excluded, whether from the parties or anywhere else, but for a real change many must come from outside party politics. Our people must be free of the last delusion that any of the parties alone or in coalition can do it. What have they to offer? Labour in its latest document appeared ready to control everything except what matters most: wages and the money supply. Well may R. Crossman write in the Times 28.2.73: "It is quite possible that we shall have to accept something like the German experience" of seeing "the Deutsche Mark lose its value twice in a lifetime." He should know. Anyone who believes that Labour can meet this problem will believe anything.

Then we have the grand coalition of the Moggs and the mugs brightly promoted in *The Times*, and stimulated by the victory of that good European, R. Taverne, in another early effort of the electorate at easy escape from a failing system. Yet it takes a number of swallows to make a summer even in Fleet Street sunshine. My experience as an Independent in the Conservative stronghold of Harrow was very similar. The full weight of the party machine was defeated by a two to one vote and victory was repeated at the next Election; yet it changed nothing.

The suggestion of a centre party faintly reflects a picture of half a century ago when the Press after the first war gave this name to a group of 150 ex-service M.Ps whose joint secretaries were C. Coote and O. Mosley. The wooing of this movement by W. S. Churchill and F. E. Smith was almost as assiduous, but not quite so ardent as the courtship of R. Jenkins by B. Levin. History sometimes repeats itself in the smoother periods of our island story, but the personnel is a little different. When things get rough no permutations of existing and hitherto responsible parties can meet the situation, particularly in the dynamism of this age of science. Debate about le centre dur contre le centre pourri can be relegated to my continental discussions of some time back. Sufficient for present British purposes to note that anyone believing our problems can be solved simply by making a mush in the middle will believe anything.

Then there is the ingenious plan to replace E. Heath when he drowns in water too deep. E. Powell is to emerge as effective, if not nominal, leader of a conservatism which saves its soul, with much advertisement for the role of redeemer by the slicker intriguers of the Labour leadership and their pink aides within the media, who may conceivably be thinking that a Tory split will sooner put their party in power, or rather the trade unions. He offers a return to the 19th century free-for-all, coupled with monetary restriction and extra taxation, which can so easily throw us back to the depression of the thirties in the absence of any plan by government then to get the economy moving again, which would be entirely against his principles. For the rest he wants Britain outside Europe, and says that all countries should float their currencies individually, which in his nostalgic world would resemble the old Gold Standard in automatic effect, but in the actual world would mean competitive devaluations arranged by dirty flotations; a game which would probably end in our ultimate exclusion from the continental markets of Europe and America. E. Powell has summarised his doctrines in three resounding pronouncements: if all countries floated their currencies independently, everyone would "live happily ever after"; the Channel remains an effective "anti-tank ditch"; the innocence of the trade unions is "as white as snow". A man who believes all this will believe anything.

Britain is left with the necessity of doing something serious, and the time for small manoeuvres runs out. As a simple pedlar of ideas, my suggestion is a government limited to the duration of one Parliament, drawn from the whole nation and supplied with emergency powers as in wartime. Time presses, because the breakdown of the Bretton Woods international system leads inexorably to the long foreseen continental systems in which we must play an effective part. Meantime, new and possibly decisive ideas may not be discussed on their merits and de-merits over the media in Britain, which for all practical purposes are exclusively at the disposal of the ideas and personnel responsible for the present situation. Such characters or their prototypes – with only brief intervals in an emergency – have been in office ever since 1914, when our country was still the greatest power in the world. Time for change?

19

Truth and Decadence - Reality and Humbug

ENOUGH of Peter Pansy civilisation, we need to restore the values of manhood. It is a good measure of contemporary decadence—this belief that Ministers might possibly divulge military secrets to prostitutes, or submit to their blackmail. Would anyone have imagined that the Duke of Wellington in his frequent visits to a celebrated brothel would incidentally have betrayed his country, or would have responded to blackmail with any other retort than "publish and be damned"? Why then these wild suspicions that a Minister with the best military record in the present government might have so acted, or another Minister who possesses ability and character? The latter was reported to say that in the event of blackmail he would have gone straight to the police, and in such an action he would have been Mr. X and the blackmailer would have been liable for anything up to 14 years in jail. In not believing a word about betrayal or yielding to blackmail, I write with complete impartiality, having never had the slightest interest in prostitutes; not a virtue, but a matter of taste.

What then are the real facts and values of this affair? They are that most politicians talk too much, but there is no evidence that the men in question talked at all. In matters of national security no one should be told anything that he need not know. Even close colleagues should be told no more than is necessary to efficiency in their jobs. No Minister has the right to tell wife or friend anything about his work. This is no question of morality, simply of discretion and of loyalty to the country.

Fornicators are often better colleagues than drunkards; they have some practice in keeping their wits about them: e.g. the

Last Words : Broadsheets 1970-1980

first Duke of Marlborough—far and away the greatest military genius our country has produced—who took a snap decision to make a hasty and dangerous exit through the bedroom window of the King's mistress on the unexpected arrival of her royal lover; he is reputed thereby to have earned £5,000 from the grateful lady, quite worth having in those days and adequate to found the fortunes of a remarkable family. "At twenty he sold his vigour and his beauty, at 60 his glory and his genius", commented Macaulay, in the latter respect unfairly. If present values— alternating between a roll in the permissive manure heap and the febrile hysteria of a repressive Puritanism— had always prevailed, Britain would have been deprived of some outstanding services.

Our most eminent historian has reckoned that at least seven British Prime Ministers have committed adultery; probably an underestimate. Certainly our leader of the First World War was among them, but nobody could conceive Lloyd George blabbing the nation's secrets to a woman. He was apparently endowed with what I regard as a happy gift of nature, liking only his own kind of women, but no one would imagine that under any stress of circumstance or passion that clear intellect and strong will would have divulged what mattered. Idle chatter of the dinner table is left to the degeneracy of the puritan tradition which couples sexual abstinence with too much eaten and too much drunk. The athletic way of life essential to all great achievement is foreign to such characters.

Lloyd George shocked many people, and things he did were sometimes indefensible. Yet I was personally far more shocked to read of letters written to a young woman at the Cabinet table by Mr. Asquith, for whose mind and character despite all political differences I had the warmest regard. It is true that this girl was of his own kind, had some beauty, wit, character, and in the event a proved discretion; also there is apparently no evidence of any physical relationship. The astounding fact remains that he wrote to her secrets in the middle of a war when men's lives were at stake. Such action is to me so inconceivable that this fine intellect appeared then to enter the realms of madness. If the life of men and nations had not been in question he might conceivably have made—mutatis mutandis —the classic defence of Aristotle in far more compromising circumstances. When tutor to the young King Alexander the Great he was reputed to have been surprised by the monarch in what is now regarded by contemporary continental opinion as one of our odd island fashions—crawling on all fours, saddled and bridled, being ridden by one young woman and walloped by another. The great philosopher without a moment's loss of composure is reported to have drawn the appropriate moral for his pupil: your Majesty will observe, and be warned by the straits to which passion can reduce even the foremost of human intellects. Which is worse?—a perverted philosopher risking nothing but his own dignity in a private exercise, or a chaste Prime Minister committing an indiscretion in the middle of a war when lives of men and nations are in the balance?

This is a brutally frank article and it is deliberately designed to draw a conclusion. It is not the varying moralities or immoralities which matter —these things have always occurred in human nature and will recur in the foreseeable future—it is this sheer, silly frivolity in serious affairs which really matter. Boozing and gassing around the town—as most politicians do—is far more a waste of time, far worse for health, energy and judgment than the "casual relationships" for which the distinguished soldier and Minister and his gifted colleague have been compelled to resign.

Certainly a strong Prime Minister should insist that his colleagues not only guard their secrets but should lead serious, dedicated lives while in the service of the nation. He should demand of them dignity in their public behaviour, but their physical and mental fitness, not their beds, are his concern. He may reasonably require that they waste no time in private frivolities, conventional or unconventional, worthy or wicked, but should live in the style of serious men of action throughout history: "ask of me anything but time" said Bonaparte. Men called to the supreme duty of government for a few years of their lives are in this respect in

Last Words : Broadsheets 1970-1980

a different category to those who spend a lifetime in normal occupations; it is not a question of morality but of time lost which belongs to the country. In the matter of general morals a Prime Minister's chief, possibly his only duty is to guard with the severest measures the young of both sexes from corruption, and above all ruthlessly to extirpate the drug menace.

All this uproar is a symptom not of propriety but of decadence. These are not the values of mature manhood but of senile womanhood. This alternation between a permissive squalor and a ridiculous Puritanism is liable to make us the laughing stock of the western world. At one moment scampering round in a frenzy of sexual licence like a poodle in a fit, at the next sitting up and wagging goody-goody tails in the hope of a few left-over Victorian biscuits—this is not England. Moral or immoral, let us be men again. It was puritan repression which originally led to the degraded absurdity of the permissive orgy. They are two sides of the same medal: turn one over and you get the other. We need again balance and firmness of character, and a just sense of a great mission in the world.

The real disaster in this situation is preoccupation with the trivial and evasion of the serious. Soviet agents like Maclean are planted in the heart of the Foreign Office, and the men who protected them are still unexposed by the brothel-peeping security services. Violent crime increases with a threat of potential disorder on a considerable scale in any change of the economic situation. The response of government is virtually to confine the possession of guns to the gangsters who can always obtain them, while denying a national police force equipped and armed to deal with anything more modern than a local highwayman on a horse.

What really shocks the people—and rightly—is not so much the peculiar antics of politicians in obscure bedrooms as the enormous disparities of industrial and financial reward. When the earnings of the workers are so severely and at present necessarily limited, the spivs, speculators, pop-stars, wide boys, manipulators, or whatever they are called in current jargon are free to amass immense fortunes without noteworthy effort. Government kicked into action against its principles by incipient crisis has but one clear desire - to discard its new and unwelcome responsibilities as soon as possible. The fact is never faced that modern government must either give a continuous economic lead or in effect cease to be a government.

Recognising the facts of a new age involves two actions which are anathema to the present political escapism of all parties. The first is that government should be given by Parliament power of rapid action in a continually changing situation, subject always to its power of dismissal by vote of censure. The second is that government must have power to intervene not only negatively but positively in determining the main lines of reward, with the purpose of securing fair treatment for those of value to the nation and of checking its exploitation. To feed the people with the dry bread and dull circus of petty scandal while vast abuses are derisively flaunted, can finally evoke from them, those decisive words of British history: "let you be gone, and let you make haste."

20

Britains Situation and What To Do About It?

A WIDE CHOICE may soon confront our British people: ignominious failure or great achievement. It is worth at least some contingency planning in advance. This situation will not arise if the Government is right that all is for the best in the best of all possible worlds, because the financial trick of a depreciating exchange and undervalued pound will give us an artificial competitive advantage which others will indefinitely permit without retaliation. If the consensus of expert opinion be right that real life will not always be so easy, things can go desperately wrong. A major decision will then be necessary in a hurry, and this brief attempt at "go" may be followed by a "stop" which can be deadly to British life as a great people. Before hysteria of pessimism succeeds euphoria of folly we should face the facts.

The inflation which threatens to wreck national life with continually rising prices can only be met by limiting both the money supply and individual rewards. It is untrue to say that either money or wages are the whole problem, and it is also untrue to say the subject is so mysterious that it cannot be explained to the people. A government capable both of decision and clarity can define the basic facts in a manner which can be understood, and can convince. If in crude example production is 100 and the money supply 100, prices are doubled if production remains 100 and the money supply becomes 200. Quantity theory can be reduced to terms so elementary, and complementary factors like velocity or recent complexities of calculation are irrelevant to this basic comprehension. If in equally hypothetical figures of simple illustration the money supply is 100 and the trade unions' share 60, that share becomes more disproportionate if money

Britains Situation and What To Do About It

is reduced from 100 to 80 and the 60 remains constant. All deliberately simplistic but basically true, and possible to explain on any television screen or platform by anyone with any capacity for popular exposition.

It is not difficult to show that action both in the sphere of money supply and wages is necessary. The question of undue profit will be all too effectively dealt with by limiting the money supply whose excess has resulted in the present orgy of anti-social profiteering. The danger is exactly the opposite. If the advocates of simply deflating and taxing had their way we should be thrown back abruptly into the depression of the thirties, and being bound fast by their free market theories they would not be able to do a thing about it. We should wallow again in the deep donkey trough of a true blue recession.

When the inflation is ended it will be necessary to move the economy forward again on a stable price level. This will require action in the public sector, but the question remains which public sector? At present lame dogs are helped over obsolete stiles by pouring out public funds of bank-created money which are largely responsible for the present inflation. Here indeed is a case for letting market forces operate and allowing these industries to sink or swim. But this would add to the unemployment following the end of inflation unless government is ready with creative works on a great scale in its true sphere, operations of modern national necessity which are too big for private enterprise.

This situation should be regarded not as an unavoidable disaster but as a great opportunity. Britain can emerge from this challenge as a modern state ready to take its place in Europe and compete with the world. Yet it would be a lie to say that from the present depth it can be done without effort and even sacrifice. We are fortunate that blood is not demanded, but much sweat and even some tears will be required. So much folly invites a sequence of some sorrow. Britain will need an effort almost equivalent to wartime, and our constitution should summon a government

Last Words : Broadsheets 1970-1980

drawn from the whole nation for the four-year lifetime of one Parliament. The British people may be asked for a period to be as serious and dedicated in peace as they are in war.

Such action can be the great way out. What is the small alternative, the ignoble choice? The first reaction of present thinking is to scrap the major projects which can link Britain with the modern world. The Channel Tunnel (or bridge), Maplin and Concorde are canvassed as the first victims of the next "stop". We are to turn our back on Europe and the future to buy the decrepit a few years or months of failing life. Far be it for anyone outside government to assign priorities in these technical questions, for my experience of government both changed preconceptions and suggested new and larger possibilities. Yet it seems incredible to be so concerned to get a few tycoons to New York in time for lunch rather than supper at the cost of breaking so many windows, while stifling the hover-train which could rapidly and happily diffuse our people throughout Europe on business or holiday made possible by British scientists who lead the world. Maybe government is inhibited by lack of preliminary thought in default not of a small "think-tank" but of the comprehensive planning staff which I vainly advocated during and since my time in government.

There is however a bright clarity in one outstanding fact. Britain needs a new infrastructure to live as a modern country. The end of the housing shortage and slum disgrace in national action with all the energy of an operation of war, strong incentive for the essential of industrial re-equipment with up-to-date machinery, the cleansing of pollution, the effective assistance of medical research to meet such scourges as cancer, the adequate defence of our country, the general support of science to draw back to the motherland some of the best brains in the world which are British—this vital preparation for re-entry in the modern world is worth effort and sacrifice. Such achievement is worth four years' hard work in which we should all be ready temporarily to reduce our consumption, tighten our belts together and give our all to restore Britain to our true position in a new age. I believe that our people in real crisis are still capable of greatness. What is the alternative to such an effort of the united nation? It is party warfare now more than ever like a children's game.

Before the need for serious effort is faced the electors will probably seek every chance of easy escape from reality. A continuance of illusion is still most likely to result in the failure of Conservatism after one gallant European effort, followed by a final and catastrophic experience of a Labour government obviously inadequate to the situation. This is rendered the more likely by Mr. Powell—walking delicately and speaking with a couple of extra plums in his mouth— who indicates to his supporters that they might vote for Labour with the doubtful effect of keeping Britain out of Europe but with the certain consequence of opening the door to coloured immigration. The issue which first brought him to public notice and lifted him from a 5 per cent vote of the Tory Parliamentary party to be a dangerous challenger to Mr. Heath, is apparently in this manoeuvre to be lightly discarded. That always inviting target— the broad posterior of the Powellite nonsense with head in sand—may be left on this occasion with the poignant query: when we "all float together" are we really "all living happily ever after"?

Shall Britain sink in the squalid squabble of small men?—or are our people still ready for a great response to a great challenge? The vital life of our country is still there—scientists, technicians, business managers, experienced trade union leaders and some still on the shop-floor but ready for the board-room, still the finest Civil Service in the world, the flower of universities, certainly a number of good and honest politicians, realistic and determined soldiers, sailors and air-men. They must come together in dedication to the rebirth of a nation.

21

World Food Prices and E.E.C. Agriculture

IT IS UNTRUE that inflation cannot be cured, but it is true that no single party can do it. A government of national concentration as in wartime is necessary to the major operation described in my last broadsheet: limiting the money supply and individual reward to the potential of production, then moving the economy forward again on a stable price level. The initial shock of ending inflation will be great and the subsequent effort of recovery and renewed growth will require exceptional determination and energy in government. A renaissance of the national will to live and to live greatly must be evoked from a people awakened by crisis. The parties and their leaders are quite right frankly to admit they cannot do it, and in fairness it should reciprocally be admitted that it cannot be done until the people feel the full effects of the mistakes the parties have made. The time is not yet, but it may be near. Meantime it is defeatist and demoralising to declare it is physically impossible to overcome inflation, when the inhibition is entirely political. The parties dare not make the attempt and the people in the inflationary hallucination of perpetual prosperity would not stand it.

Bust can follow, either when the domestic inflation gets right out of hand or our competitors are obliged to defend themselves against an effectively devalued pound. Both are now distinct possibilities: vide an increase in the money supply at an annual rate of 41.4 per cent in the last published figures, and of 15.4 per cent in wages; also the difficulties into which our continental neighbours have recently been thrown by our exports enjoying the bonus of an undervalued currency. The delicate exercise of everyone at the same time trying to sell more than they buy has

World Food Prices and E.E.C. Agriculture

not been perfected even in the clear air of Nairobi, and it will further be complicated by an event which like many decisive facts of history has passed almost unnoticed. The external trade of America is now moving from deficit to surplus, and the flood of paper dollars on which all floated happily until they nearly drowned in consequent inflation may now yield to a tempest of exports blown on to world markets by an undervalued dollar. The relatively sober continent of Europe has observed that the Anglo-Americans have learned a new game, and is considering how to meet the situation. The resulting bucket of cold water may bring to the steady head of England the bracing thought that we must at length put our own house in order.

How to put our own house in order by action mentioned above has been discussed in some detail so often in these broadsheets that repetition would be redundant and tedious. The immediate task is to examine the alibi of the parties that they are the helpless victims of world prices. "External factors", as Mr. Attlee used to call them, are the continual excuse for doing nothing at home. What they cannot do is made the reason for not doing what they can do. Action at home by decision of the British people can be relatively rapid, though painful; it would still be necessary even if world prices corrected themselves. Action in face of world price movements must be slower because it involves the persuasion of other people. It is not impossible if we can arouse the Europeans to save themselves; a process which requires Britain as accelerator to the European engine rather than brake on the wheel.

Europe today is nearly self-sufficient in the production of temperate foodstuffs and this independence of world prices could be made complete. We will consider why the event would be a benefit rather than a detriment to the rest of the world. First let the rout of the European negative be regarded, the final discomfort of the claim that Britain would be ruined by buying dear food in Europe rather than cheap food on world markets. *The Daily Telegraph* reported (15.8.73) that "the hard wheat price on the world market now stands at £142 per ton

Last Words : Broadsheets 1970-1980

compared with £70 as the average price on the E.E.C. internal market". Since then the world price has continued to fluctuate, though the disparity has been less extreme. This is indeed a sharp setback for the "long-eared band" of European destruction and desecration, the odd assortment of Whigs called Tories and Little England socialists so clearly belonging to the 19th century. They have considerable influence because they are still without effective answer on the media, but are now reduced by hard facts to saying that perhaps prices on the oscillating world market may one day again be cheaper than E.E.C. prices. What a prospect for people who want to know what the money in their pockets is going to buy, and what a paradise for the speculators who get their pickings from chaos. Is not the lesson learnt at last that we need a stable price level for the basic necessities of life against which we can build a high wage system by mass production for an assured market; already a proved possibility. The prime need is that people should have the purchasing power to buy what they want in conditions of stability and security.

Europe self-sufficient in food could remedy with agreement most of the disabilities of the present system. Personally I have always preferred the relative simplicities of British thinking on this subject to the Latin complexities of the E.E.C. arrangements. Such things as the overproduction of butter and underproduction of meat can be corrected directly by timely adjustment of price levels, though farming is a long-term business as all of us who have been actively engaged in agriculture are all too well aware. Many mistakes could have been avoided if Britain had been a foundation member rather than a latecomer. Now we must bear in mind the penetrating sarcasm of Monsieur Reynaud: "when we have built the house you may possibly consent to occupy a best room of your own design". We must also reflect that to join a club and promptly to place a bomb in the basement is neither honourable nor advantageous. Agriculture with a large working population on the land is the sound and healthy basis of continental life. To blow up that foundation would be a disaster for us all. A friend of mine who is one of the main grain dealers of France tells me that many of his small farmers have lived and worked as a family on the same piece of land for over a thousand years. It would not contribute to the health and stability of either France or Germany if such people were thrown rapidly and in large numbers into the unemployment queues of the towns during a potential industrial crisis. Already the drive from the land has proceeded for years at an almost dangerous speed, and a drastic acceleration can bring disaster. Far better at last to face the fact that the towns owe agriculture a decent living —Britain included—and can pay for it with the higher wages a large and assured industrial market can provide. The rationalisation of large-scale farming on good land with ever-increasing production is in any case coming apace, but it is better in addition to have a system of grants for the small farmers on poor land than to depopulate the countryside and depend for much on external speculation. Agriculture brings not only the present means of life, but health, stability and security to the future life of our Europe.

The charge will be brought that this is a protectionist system aiming at European self-sufficiency. I plead guilty not only to seeking insulation from the predatory speculation of world chaos but also to desiring even a surplus of food production in Europe for a most beneficent purpose. We have bragged for years about feeding the hungry of the world and have done precious little about it. A European surplus can be realised by this system and can be used to make good many words, at last with an effective deed. Further, we can not only save ourselves and do our own good work, but can encourage others by our example. America and the British Dominions might be persuaded to join with us in the greatest act of charity the world has yet seen, and might even agree to carry the cost on a combined budget. There are many possibilities when we substitute great policies for small bargains and firm action for empty words. In the nocturnal haggling of coming months my advice to all negotiators is: raise the sights to further and larger targets.

22

European Government - Problems and Dangers

ANY fool can deflate, just as any fool can inflate: the real question is what to do after that. It is easy enough by sharply reducing the money supply to throw Britain back into the depression of the thirties. The odd idea exists in some circles that after the creation of enough bankruptcies and unemployment the situation will then cure itself. Those who had to face the facts in the thirties know better. It has since been generally admitted that my constructive proposals in the government of that period would in the prevailing conditions have moved the economy forward again. When they were rejected things went from bad to worse in a vicious circle of industrial stagnation and rising unemployment. After deflation there was not a flicker of recovery. British government lay helpless, until floated off the rocks neither by devaluation nor even by Roosevelt's doubling of the price of gold which had only brief effect, but ultimately by the rearmament boom and the Second World War. In the economic sense they were only rescued from deflation by another inflation.

The present period is further complicated by two new factors. The first is the much increased power of certain key trade unions. The old Tory remedy of knocking the economy flat as the simplest means of bashing the trade unions—curiously implemented by the Labour leaders—will no longer work, because some of these organisations have become so strong that they can still hold the State up to ransom even in face of massive unemployment in the rest of industry. It is not only necessary for government to restrict the presently inflated money supply and to have constructive measures ready to move the economy forward again at the end of the inflation, not in a public sector subsidising obsolete or inefficient industries but rather in undertakings too large for private enterprise which can give the country a modern infrastructure. It is also vital for government to present an incomes policy which evokes public support by being manifestly fair to all, and which it has the will to enforce with power of law supported by strength of State.

The second new factor in the modern situation is the runaway boom in world prices of food stuffs and raw materials. We have moved from the deflationary world of the thirties to the inflationary world of the seventies. Prices fluctuate wildly and more than ever the speculators rule the international system, more than ever the interest of such finance conflicts with the interest both of producer and consumer. Yesterday prices in the EEC were considerably above world prices, which gave every politician who could not see above or beyond the muddle of the butter surplus a powerful appeal to all who could only feel through the pocket, unfortunately the case of everyone in days of soaring prices. Today world prices are substantially above EEC prices, and myopic politicians find themselves on a butter slide to silence. It becomes yet clearer that we shall be tied forever to the speculative insanity of world chaos if we cannot create a viable area where government elected by the people can enable full production equated by fair consumption on the steady price level of a stable system. This means Europe, and it soon means European government.

Europe and Watergate

Economic problems can only be solved within Europe, and world dangers can only be faced by European government. It was a suggestion to awaken the dead or even a somnolent politician that the life of each of our helpless European countries might have recently depended on the vagaries of Watergate. It was probably untrue that the American "alert", which took the world to the brink of war, was occasioned by need to cover up an American domestic situation—there were clearly other reasons,

Last Words : Broadsheets 1970-1980

right or wrong, of international import—but a situation of that kind could occur in the future so long as an impotent Europe clings to the hand of America or licks the boot of Russia. All this indeed reduces to the dimension of the comic if it were not so profoundly dangerous and tragic, the now pathetic argument that we are losing our national sovereignty by entering effectively into Europe. Long since, in NATO, we have committed ourselves to instant war under American command at the behest of others. The whole question of survival as a country has now passed right out of British hands.

It is all very well in such conditions of potential war to complain that the Americans had not consulted every European partner—how on earth could they in a serious situation? Is it really suggested that if the Russians had ordered a partial mobilisation, the Americans should run round the lot of us rallying the determined and consoling the dithering before they took any corresponding action to meet it? Anyone who knows the ABC of war is aware that speed and often secrecy are of the essence, and that such delays are right out of the question when conflict is imminent. Are we indeed to understand from the recent parliamentary debate that in some future possibility of America and Russia being locked in a survival struggle all eyes will be fixed on Mr. Callaghan waving the starting flag or raising the monitory finger which beckons stop?

Yet of course it is for all European countries a situation of insupportable risk and intolerable national humiliation to have our countries used as military bases and therefore to be inevitably involved in war for the sake of any American adventure in which we may not have the slightest interest and with which we may not even feel agreement. This is the present dilemma of Europe: either lie helpless and unprotected at the feet of Russia or be simply the tail of a dog which may go mad. There is only one answer: European government which can speak rapidly and effectively in the name of all Europe and can with combined strength acquire the might to make that voice effective.

European Government - Problems and Dangers

Europe's Life or Death Question

Where would America be today if the Pentagon had to secure the consent of every State governor before taking any essential step in national defence, because central authority was lacking? Where would America be today if each of its states had its own currency and was trying to win against each of the others a favourable balance of payments by competitive devaluations? Would America still be able to lead the world in science and industry, and match the military might of Russia, despite every complexity, absurdity and tragedy of its politics? Would it be able to face the Soviets whose whole economy is geared to and sacrificed to the military machine, if the heads of all its states had to meet to define a common position in every crisis? The fault of our dear Europeans lies not in their diverse politics and local customs, but in their deep, archaic national divisions, that they are underlings to the super powers.

We Europeans have lost already the power to decide whether we live or die. Cannot we then take the risk of holding our own in democratic debate with fellow Europeans to decide fiscal and economic questions of common interest just as we do in our individual parliaments today? European parliament elected by the whole people of our continent—which becomes our country—can create and control an European government which could take back into our hands the question of life or death. It is true that we have not the armaments to match the super powers, but we already have enough to inflict on any assailant damage unacceptable to any sane government. The combined industrial strength of Europe can certainly much increase it before the finally inevitable withdrawal of the Americans, who might be more than willing to expedite that release by trading arms to a European government strong and reliable enough to stand true to our alliance if either be attacked. Detente could follow the emergence of European experience and traditional wisdom between the younger contestants. Disarmament agreement is not impossible when Russia is so preoccupied with its own industrial development that it is now reported to borrow for this purpose enough from America to require half its export earnings in debt service by 1980. Whether America thereby pays Danegeld for the equipment of a potential enemy or pacifies the world, it gives us time to make Europe, and then to pursue a policy which in strength so clearly seeks peace with both West and East that it can hold the balance of the globe.

This danger should indeed "gleam like sunshine to the eyes of the brave", for it illuminates the path of necessity, the road to Europe. Time presses, and all lesser things should be surpassed: we must unite to make Europe. Nothing is lacking except the will of the European peoples, and in crisis this can be aroused by voices which are clear and faith which is strong.

23

Government with Wartime Power to Act

A GOVERNMENT drawn from the whole nation is required, with wartime power to act. We need the best of politics, business, trade unions, science, universities and services of the Crown in a government to meet crisis. They should have freedom to act rapidly in a changing and menacing situation, subject to the right of a newly elected Parliament to dismiss them any day by vote of censure. Government and Parliament should largely consist of men and women usually unconcerned with a political career, but ready to serve our country for the five-year life of one Parliament in order to save the present and secure the future. That dedication would enable them to act without fear or favour, because they would be ready to retire when their task was done. Normality could then return as at the end of a war to which this situation in gravity and danger is entirely comparable.

Before the nation braces itself for such a decision it is possible, and indeed probable that it will seek the easy way out by an election which will return a party or coalition government again named national. This will waste time and change nothing, because it will consist of men and parties who have failed already; zero plus zero remains a nullity. There are good men among them with valuable administrative experience, and some of the political rank and file are the salt of the earth, but the parties have neither the character nor the policy for a solution. Regard the present situation and reflect that at the end of the first war our country was still the greatest power in the world. Since then the Conservative Party has been in power for two thirds of the time and the Labour Party has had a very fair opportunity to show what it could do. Liberalism re-enters refreshed after long exclusion with new ideas and faces, but few would entrust to those slender shoulders alone the crushing weight of this new world. We need for the testing period not the proved weakness of the parties but the latent strength of the whole nation expressed in a majority decision to live and to live greatly.

A great recovery is possible because the disaster is due not to the blows of fate but to political mistakes. This is not wisdom after the event, because for years I have said it would happen and have challenged each error with a constructive alternative. The only unforeseeable factor in the present situation was the sudden decision of the long ill-treated Arabs to use their oil weapon; this was precipitated by the Middle East war. But even this surprise would have been surmounted if we had developed our own resources instead of remaining tied to the international financial system which now collapses. We failed to produce enough fuel from our own coal, or from the oil sands of Alberta despite repeated Canadian offers which have now been taken up by America, or from the sugar of Jamaica whose ruin brought the immigrants to Britain. The reason given was that production at that time would have been more expensive than free market competition within the world costing system would permit. The Empire could always have easily solved the problem and even our island alone could have done much, while a truly united Europe with combined will and resources could in fair dealing have secured its fuel supply with consummate ease. These policies I suggested successively over years, and now mention not to cry over spilt milk, or even spilt blood, but to point to new ways.

Recrimination is useless and should stop for good: the question is what to do now? The first answer is to change from a negative to a positive. A dynamic policy must replace "prices and incomes" with its frozen "phase 3", which sits inert before disaster like a rabbit in front of a boa-constrictor. Government must give continuous economic leadership with a statutory wage-price mechanism which has force of law supported by full power of State. The world changes and differentials must also change in favour of those who have value and have always been badly treated; in this I state no new opinion. The old Tory remedy of deflation and free market forces will not work, because it will still leave key trade unions in an all-powerful position despite massive bankruptcy and unemployment of others, and will still leave a few speculative financiers on top of the powerless State. The country will still belong not to its people but to those who carry the economic guns. The recently inflated money supply must of course be curtailed to the potential of production, but government must not then let industry lie derelict in the depression of the thirties. It must be ready to intervene with constructive measures which move the economy forward again and give the country a modern infrastructure.

Government should be armed by the electorate with power to decide who gets what, and, after that majority decision, he who will not work shall not be supported by the State when his own money is exhausted. Trade union funds should be inviolate for their normal and beneficent purposes, but not for support of strikes against wages settled by law. The basic fact is that we have reached the point where someone must decide and act, and the only legitimate authority is government drawn from the whole nation and given requisite power by the people, subject to control and, if necessary, dismissal by their elected Parliament. Naturally such government will seek detailed advice from the whole nation, and particularly from trade unions and employers, but in wartime conditions of a siege economy it must have power, for the lifetime of one Parliament, when necessary to settle wages, profit, rent and interest. In the wider context of Europe normality can return, but our country needs first to be made fit.

The second answer is to change from a negative to a positive in our European policy. Enough of penny-wise, pound foolish; a great policy which unites must replace the small haggle which divides. Those who say get out, must explain how they will sell 37 per cent of our manufactures abroad in face of the continental systems which will replace the present breakdown of the international system. If our goods are excluded from Europe and America, where will we sell enough to buy raw materials and sufficient food - even when we have fully developed our own agriculture? The present hope is apparently that slick financial tricks will enable us to live as well on the Arab surplus as we did on the American deficit.

What a position for a great people - and does anyone in his senses think it will long last? The alternative is united action in the common interest and in the common purposes of Europe. The economic weight and persuasive power of a truly united Europe can achieve anything. Apart from the internal market and its enormous resources, who can withstand the declaration: Europe buys from those who buy from Europe, and Europe supplies those who supply Europe? We can again be a great power, and the English genius, scientific, industrial and financial will have a genuine base of strength from which to operate for its own benefit and that of all Europe. The skill and goodwill of the British people will at last be free to earn what they deserve in their own land, without servitude to external forces or disruption from world chaos. We approach the hour of decision: may our people's choice be wise and resolute.

24

The Election Observed – What Chance for Reality?

TO BE back in England watching every move of the election has been a revealing experience. The only decisive result is that the combined Conservative and Liberal vote is an overwhelming endorsement of entry into Europe, which was made a very live issue. The rest merely extends and exacerbates the existing confusion. An evident but still incipient search of many people for new measures and new men has not yet produced clarity. The question remains: what to do now, what means are left to do it, when will the developing crisis awaken our people to support the necessary action by willing the means as well as desiring the end.

The first necessity is government supplied by Parliament with authority to act rapidly in a continually changing situation. The fact that everything cannot be foreseen has so far only provided excuses for the responsible parties. Rather it should urge the necessity of giving government both the means of rapid action and of foresight on which effective decision depends. This postulates an Enabling Act as in wartime, and a general staff of government planning to meet all possible contingencies. Such a basic requirement of all serious organisation should not only obviate minor muddles in calculation which have recently brought the country to the brink of industrial catastrophe, but should also equip government with clarity and precision to face the larger problems of a mobile and dangerous period. An absolute power of parliament to dismiss government at any time by vote of censure should assuage the fears of those who prefer death by inertia to the risks of movement.

Last Words : Broadsheets 1970-1980

Most recent mistakes and hesitations have arisen in circumstances which could clearly be foreseen, and all parties still appear to have a partial rather than comprehensive view of these events. The paramount problem of inflation has to be met in all three particulars: demand-pull, cost-push, and world price movements. The first two must both be more firmly treated, and the third should not be an alibi for failure but an inspiration for larger policies. Demand-pull inflation was inevitable when maximal hope of growth was 5 per cent per annum and the increase of the money supply was at the rate of over 25 per cent. Such elementary inflation is not compulsory even when bankrupt concerns seek to repay their creditors in depreciating currency. Cost-push inflation must also be met by statutory policy because some modern trade unions are still strong enough to hold the country up to ransom even in deflationary conditions. But use of a real wage-price mechanism should be positive in deciding new relativities rather than negative in a universal freeze irrespective of merit.

World price fluctuations can only be met by entry into a viable area with effective authority. This means Europe, with a steady drive toward European government. The house-wife can only be saved from the wildly fluctuating prices of a speculative world by government of an area extensive enough to be largely independent of such movements and therefore capable of maintaining a stable price level against which reward, pensions and social services can be raised as science increases the power to produce. The shopping-basket depends on wider concepts than hanging it on the parish pump, and this can be explained in adequate detail on television by anyone who has the capacity to simplify and to mass meetings, by any who has had the practice the parties now lack. We must see the problem clearly, and also see it whole.

This premonitory breakdown of the old party system suggests that in real crisis a new majority can be found in the country for effort as well as for sacrifice, for sweat more than tears, for the energy of manhood rather than the passivity of decadence. The

The Election Observed - What Chance for Reality

whole people should be constantly consulted by government, and minorities should be treated with every possible consideration, but in the end democracy is a matter of majority decision if the nation is not to die of frustration. Paralysis should not be disguised as moderation in a competition of dear little chaps to explain how moderate they are. It soon becomes clear that their performances have been and will be even more moderate than they are themselves. The stature of most of them in relation to the problem is all too evident. A great age needs rather a balanced dynamism of character to do what the country requires and the people desire.

A new determination of our people to live, and to live greatly, could best be expressed in an assembly of the nation ready to serve in Parliament for the duration of a crisis equivalent to war. They would be asked to support a government also drawn from the whole nation: the best of politics, business, trade unions, universities, civil and defence services, particularly science. Parliament might then eliminate the pretence of conducting every detail, and act rather as shareholders of the nation controlling directors whom they could dismiss by vote at any time. This would indeed permit the best, most vital and experienced so to serve, because they could continue in their normal occupations and yet be M.P.s who met for a week about six times a year in televised debates which promote sobriety. They would know more of the real life of the country than can be learned by loitering in the lobbies or sitting in Whitehall, and would be a true link between government and people; each would thus always know what the other was doing and thinking. The great indispensable institution of Parliament would be transmuted from a talk-shop into a work-shop.

How many nonsense elections must occur before such a majority can emerge in the country and be returned to Parliament? The answer may yet be clear: when the degree of crisis is sufficient to awaken our people, always slow to start, always resolute when they do. Such character will be necessary to meet the shock of real policies when the smooth world of make believe has failed. No one but a fool seeks tough measures until all other means have been tried with infinite patience. Yet already it is widely admitted that we cannot leave the complexities of the twentieth century to the obsolescence of the nineteenth century free market, and the intricacies of modern industrial relativities to the crudities of the dog-fight. If government has to intervene and act, give it the power to do so properly and completely. If wages—and much else in crisis—are fixed by law, let the law be enforced. Do not pay supplementary benefits to subsidise strikes against the law. Do not even allow trade union funds to be used in support of strikes against the law, but only for other purposes of their members in continually expanding and beneficent activities. Strikes would not last long if funds were frozen, and women and children were fed directly by improvised organisation until men again assumed their family obligations and obeyed the law. Such action would have the authority of a parliamentary majority implementing the frequently expressed desire of the people—including trade unionists—for industrial anarchy to be replaced by government leadership.

Action must be positive rather than negative, because some must get more and others less. Miners, nurses, doctors, dustmen, scientists should long ago have had more, while speculators and some trade unions—wielding more power than the weak State—should have less. Does this mean strong government—yes, of course, it does. If the national cart is to be pulled out of the bog it needs a strong horse to do it. Will it mean a row?—yes, quite possibly. Government should do its best to avoid it with every resource of gentle persuasion, but should be ready to meet it. This needs, in addition to our present admirable police force, a new national police trained to deal with riot by modern and scientific methods which kill no one. We in the professional army were trained to win by shooting, and to win quickly. That is why an army should never be used in civil disturbance except as a last resort; to be gentle is bad for the army, and to be rough is bad for the State.

The Election Observed - What Chance for Reality

The moderation of this nation can only be guarded by the readiness of government to act before extreme situations arise: first to do in time what is necessary and the people want done, second to secure their fullest possible participation in every sphere of national and industrial life from grassroots to government, third to stop disorder firmly and timely before it spreads as a disease throughout the land. It is work the country wants done, but many still fear giving any government the power to do it. The answer is complete parliamentary control by men and women who would serve for the duration of crisis, but would be content to return whence they came when their task was done. Happy games for easy times, and serious people for serious times: a good English tradition.

25

A New Majority? or Luck Thrown Away Again?

SOME trade union leaders declare the intention of bringing down a government, and succeed. A General Election impelled by industrial disorder then causes a minority government with 38 per cent, of the votes recorded. The result is the reversal of the two main policies for which 58.4 per cent, of the electorate have voted. For it cannot be denied that both the Conservative and Liberal parties stood for our entry into Europe and for a statutory incomes policy. When the threat of breaking the law can bring down a government the next administration quickly falls into line. An actual premium was put on lawlessness by the Labour Government's amnesty for illegal immigrants, which was neither the declared intention of the Labour Party nor of the belated convert to its electoral support. Other cases will be familiar: in short, the whole system has been stood on its head in a travesty of democracy. Yet euphoria of surrender has been induced by a simple handout with the promise of more to come, and this government may yet escape to electoral victory before the consequences are felt.

It is not surprising if a general feeling exists that this cannot last, and a considerable contempt arises for the whole process of contemporary politics. Yet it is not Parliament which is wrong, but some of the people inside it. They are content to work a system which is not only obsolete but now clearly frustrates the declared will of the people. A minority goes further and seeks to reduce to a screaming shambles the dignified procedure of parliamentary debate. This evokes from an opposing minority a demand for a military coup d'etat which has invariably failed during modern experience in the developed countries—for easily

A New Majority? or Luck Thrown Away Again

discernible reasons—even when large and influential armies have long been established pillars of the State. Great Britain is neither a monkey-house nor a banana republic.

The alternative is a via media in accord with British tradition, which is slowly being recognised under the pressure of events. We need a new majority drawn from the whole country, the best of politics, business, trade unions, science, universities, civil services, and defence services which can make a great contribution under the constitutional control of Parliament. The best can then serve in Parliament because they will have time to pursue their normal avocations, if this modern council of the nation only meets at necessary intervals to survey and control the work of government. The return of a government based on such a majority at a General Election can transform the whole life, psychology and morale of the nation: a true renaissance. It can be a dawn which acclaims Britain awake instead of Britain asleep. Change can come without risk, for such a fine but effective balance of national forces, in combination with the right of Parliament to dismiss government at any time by vote of censure, can lift the fear of adventure from even the most timid. A wartime power to act can do what has to be done in the period of one Parliament without chance of abuse. At last can be achieved the vital synthesis of action and liberty.

The risk of continuing along the dusty track of current failure is certainly greater than is recognised by the mass of our people, and even the initiated may underrate the danger. The slap-happy muddle of short-term political manoeuvres may easily take us out of Europe; the CBI protest was more than timely. It is no good just oafing into Europe, playing the bogus John Bull; no-one is any longer impressed, and this essentially domestic pantomime may end with Britain outside the main performance. All this merely confirms the view that the "Anglo Saxons" will at best be a nuisance and at worst a Trojan horse; therefore the quicker they are out the better, they should never have been admitted. The eager allies of this opinion within our country should be

Last Words : Broadsheets 1970-1980

asked a simple question when they say the Commonwealth is an alternative to Europe. Where will they sell 37 per cent, of our total manufactures in order to pay for the food and raw materials we must import? After the violation of a treaty Europe may virtually exclude our goods, which it can well do without, and America may retreat into the self-contained system which is always possible, rather than rest on the shifting sands of our continent. To whom will Britain then sell the vital 37 per cent?—is President Amin the answer?

The false dilemma frequently stated between Europe and America is simply a symptom of political incompetence. Open and honourable dealing first with the family and then with the partner can meet the problem. In the case of the oil surprise a vigorous initiative could have united Europe for action, and would have secured joint consultation and agreement with America for a common front. I have never found the slightest difficulty in America either on mass television or in private conference when stating the firmest of European positions. Americans would much prefer a reliable partner to a collection of helpless and hopeless satellites. They only want to take us over when we are proved to be incapable of running our own affairs. It is even possible to discuss with reason rather than petulance the suggestion that America can easily become a virtually self-contained system without any dependence on our markets, and that consequently the best method is a faithful alliance of equals in face of communism without undue and irksome economic interdependence. Most things are possible to a Britain with clear minds and great policies. What is no longer possible is the fuddled ambition to straddle three stools — Europe, Commonwealth, America—with the inevitable end of a heavy fall between them in a position all too frequently occupied by our country in recent times.

We need Europe, not only as an essential market but as the solution to our problems; even if the appeal of common origin and close relationship in millennia of history and a great culture can evoke only a limited response. We can stop domestic inflation,

A New Majority? or Luck Thrown Away Again

both demand - pull and cost - push, with strong government, but we cannot insulate ourselves from world inflation without a viable area as large as Europe in close association with Africa. Yet Britain is invited to turn from this great life to the possibly fragile hope of wallowing in a warm ooze of oil which may easily change in miscalculation to the glacial chill of death. An article in *The Economist* (6.4.74) might have cured the lightest head of the present easy optimism that North Sea discoveries will repair all errors and will obviate the need for any serious effort while we live on borrowed money. If hope is frustrated by ultimate costing within a system still dependent on world markets, or by the development of alternative fuels under the stress of new demand, we must be strong to face the consequences which already require contingency planning. If, on the other hand, the oil fortune proves an extraordinary stroke of luck—as well it may—we still need to put our house in order to take advantage of it. Even luck cannot support too heavy a burden of folly.

How often has our country been saved from the errors of politics by the unforeseen and unforeseeable gifts of science? How often has the resulting possibility of prosperity, happiness and a great civilisation been thrown away? After the fortunate invention of nuclear science Sir Winston Churchill observed: "there is a powerful feeling that but for American nuclear superiority Europe would have been reduced to satellite status" (*The Times* 2.3.55). Science then averted the consequence of policies which led to that situation. Science and technics now again give a chance to avoid the consequence of policies which would have led to national bankruptcy in default of remedies far more draconian than present politics would support. If this be luck we must not abuse it, if this be disaster we must be ready to meet it. Either the smile or the frown of destiny will require a resurgence of the nation's will. There is a tide in the affairs of men, but to take it at its height we must not linger in these depths.

26

Ireland – A political Solution Within Europe

AGREED the army must stay because we cannot tamely surrender Ulster to a disaster which might involve the whole of Ireland. Can we also agree that the Army should be given a chance to make a job of it, and that justice should be done? This means a frontier shortened and effectively closed. It also means that the initial injustice should be corrected. I wrote in this sense so long ago as 8.10.71 in Broadsheet No. 10. Since then the failure of other devices stresses the necessity for realistic action and larger policies.

The two objectives of shortening the frontier and correcting the injustice coincide. They require the implementing of the original Boundary Commission proposals which transferred much of Fermanagh and Tyrone with their Catholic populations to the south; honouring the pledge of Lloyd George to Michael Collins. The overriding military necessity of the shortest possible frontier must modify the original arrangements, which were not perfect. Then the Army could operate a method familiar to it since the South African war. The frontier can be effectively closed by two lines of wire intersected by blockhouses. Modern technology can reinforce original experience and economise man power with deterrents between the lines and the continual patrol of aircraft, helicopters, armoured cars or tanks. There is no doubt that physically the frontier could be entirely closed and that all traffic would then have to pass through military check-points on the main roads. The operation could be supported by the duly notified mining of Ulster waters accompanied by surveillance of fast armed craft in passages free to its trade.

Ireland - A political Solution Within Europe

The Army would at last have a proper chance to complete the job for two reasons: the supply of arms from outside would be stopped, and reinforcements from outside would also be stopped. Even the best regular troops have to be withdrawn from the front line and rested at frequent intervals. This lesson was clearly learnt in the first war, an event at least as trying as anything experienced since.

The I.R.A. like any other army clearly withdraws its troops and rests them in due course, possibly at some American expense, the necessary relief would be denied to them if there were no access to the south. Lack of arms and lack of rest can in time baffle even the most determined adversaries. This is war which requires a military operation, not a policeman on his beat. If the war be extended at any time on a large scale to Britain the navy would take over more of the work. All shipping from Ireland to Britain would be directed to the main ports where all entrants would be required to carry identity cards for examination. Such measures give the best chance of a military decision. Yet this is not enough; it cannot ultimately endure without adequate hope of a political solution. That hope depends like most fair prospects on a degree of union in Europe which the sterility of present policies may render remote in the opinion of many. However, the Irish are not only people of long memories but also sometimes of long foresight. They can realise from their own hard experience that protracted failure to secure the life of their desire will eventually arouse the will of the European peoples to secure the real union which alone can provide it.

The union of Europe will come, and within it the old and bitter quarrel concerning the union of Ireland can be resolved. This is conceivable some time before the complete union of Europe in the thorough achievement of three-tier government— European, national and regional - directly Britain, Ulster and Eire acquire the full sense, practical and spiritual, of being part of the European community. We can then begin to substitute designs large and modern for quarrels ancient and atavistic. This fresh thinking will be assisted by the sharp urge of discomfort in the severe arrangements present events make necessary. The pressure of the material can often aid the emergence of the ideal; evident in the union within Europe of many related peoples who already surmount the bitter divisions of history. This is a cause worthy of the devotion and dedication of which the Irish have long proved themselves capable.

The hope of ultimate solution within Europe is an absolute necessity in present despair, and can be more and more clearly defined as we approach effective union. Very soon Europe can complete its present contribution in two respects which are very diverse but both vital to the problem: the entire security of our strategic approaches in the West and a constitutional guarantee of minority and individual rights: two anxieties of British and Irish resolved. Then we must lift the quarrel out of the rut of the past into the wider context of the future. In large or small affairs all dealing is now too rigid. We have to deal with everyone who can contribute to a solution, orthodox or extreme. If this be war we have finally to deal with the men who are doing the fighting, as Lloyd George did before. But to get that settlement we have first to reduce both the area and the means of the fighting.

The methods already suggested can eliminate supply of arms and external reinforcements. They also greatly reduce the base from which guerrillas can operate. That base is the support of the civilian population. The redrawing of the boundary will transfer most of the Catholic population of Ulster to the south. It would also be wise to offer the most generous terms to the remaining Catholics in the north— notably in Belfast—to go south. Many would undoubtedly prefer to stay, but, in any case, the base of guerrilla operations would be much curtailed. Those without experience of fighting in these conditions have no idea how essential to guerrillas is their base in the support of the civilian population from which they emerge and into which they retreat. Both guerrillas and strikers depend ultimately on the support of the people, without which they are lost. Hence the success both of the I.R.A. owing to the support of the Catholic minority and of the strikers owing to the support of the Protestant majority. The prevailing defeatism is entirely wrong in believing that a General Strike in England could be equally effective, after a General Election which proved that the majority of the people were on the side of the government of the day. In those totally different conditions, firm will in government would win quickly and decisively.

Strength and peace, or weakness and war: the old choice arises in the Ulster problem. First we need the military solution: cutting off the arms and reinforcements of the adversary, and, at least, reducing his base. This is the job of the Army, and well it can do it. Police for the more normal tasks should not be recruited from either side, but should be an impartial body of experienced and seasoned men, such as Army reservists, whose duty would be not only the initial preservation of order but a guarantee to minorities of the separate way of life and civilisation they desire; the sine qua non of any ultimate peace. The cost of paying them well - and at last paying the Army well - together with the cost of generous terms for people willing to transfer - Catholics from north to south, or Protestants from south or west to north would be negligible in comparison with the cost of continuing war on a large scale. Yet when all this is done the outcome will depend on political will and skill: readiness to meet the men who can contribute anything, whether friend or foe, and the capacity to lift the savagery of conflict into the constructive thought and practical achievement of peace.

27

The Two Hysterias

Monkey House or Banana Republic

GREAT BRITAIN is neither a monkey house nor a banana republic. Yet these two hysterias - a continuing anarchy or a military coup d'etat - begin to emerge from the prevailing pessimism and almost universal defeatism. A strident minority seeks to transmute even the traditional dignity of parliament into the monkey house, and evokes from another minority the demand for a military solution which works, if at all, only in the most backward countries. A fairly exact science of politics is discernible in the events of more than fifty years which proves that in the great nations only political solutions are possible, even when they are countries with deeply established military traditions. The practical question in Britain is how to find a political answer which rests on a new reality within parliament and the constitution. The electorate clearly now moves instinctively to something beyond the crude absurdities of current party warfare. Yet a coalition of parties which have already failed will not long satisfy this demand, even with a few new ingredients from sources which are essentially the same. Crisis will soon indicate that an altogether different order of mind and will is necessary to face a situation as grave as war but more difficult to meet because it does not immediately evoke the same degree of national unity. Government will need at least a proportion of men who in one way or another have proved themselves in a background of tough experience, who have been under fire. Some will of course be found among the best of the politicians, but more should be drawn from the diverse experience of the whole nation, which includes an army under parliamentary and constitutional control.

The Two Hysterias

There will probably have to be yet another nonsense election which settles nothing, as well as deepening crisis, before the country is ready for the big change and the requisite personnel is prepared to take the risk. Yet already certain essentials are possible. To meet a really serious crisis there are three practical necessities: a credible government to convince the people that the big change can come, an electoral machine to secure that government a parliamentary majority, the support of the army in any disorder which challenges the constitution. These things are possible if the will is there; only will is now lacking. If sufficient men of proved ability and character came together, the government could be presented at any time. The electoral machine could be provided either by an old party organisation or by an improvised machine. The issue in such circumstances would be settled far more by television debate than by electoral technique, and an alternative government which could produce personalities adequate to that debate, together with six hundred candidates, would have all the facilities necessary to victory. The support of the army would be secured both by its character which is loyal to the constitution of Britain, and by the inclusion of some of its distinguished members in the government to which they could contribute a trained capacity to face danger. We who had the fortune to start life in the professional army are aware that a military education and experience of war are a good foundation for cool and determined action in great events.

A new parliament returned at a general election could contain the best of the nation because members would have time to pursue their normal life as well as attend a House of Commons which only met at regular intervals to do what is necessary. There is nothing wrong with parliament except antiquated procedure and some of the people inside it. Modern parliament should be a council of the nation which judges government by results without obsolete pretence of controlling every detail, suggests appropriate action to government from its diverse knowledge and experience, dismisses government by vote of censure if it fails in its duty or abuses liberty. The doers rather than the discards of national and industrial life would find themselves at home there, and would be able in this experience to decide whether their personal future lay in government or in industry and the various professions. The life of parliament and of the nation would again be integrated.

Such a government must of course decide in advance on the broad lines of action which it would present for the electorate's approval, and be free from the consensus illusion that every-one can agree about everything. The principle should be affirmed that under true democracy the will of the majority must prevail, while every minority is treated with all possible consideration and personal liberty is never abused. In a rapidly changing situation government should receive from parliament power of rapid action as in wartime. Mistakes would of course often be made and should at once be admitted, but in this method they can quickly be corrected. Everything cannot be foreseen in advance - the approach in this age of modern science must be pragmatic - but protracted failure or arrogance of power must be subject to swift dismissal by parliament.

All programmes should be presented to our people with humility born of the knowledge that situations change and new facts are learnt in government, but with a clear determination in their service to act rather than surrender to the pessimism of defeatism and decadence. We are faced with the paramount problem of inflation to which partial rather than comprehensive answers are usually given. It is, of course, necessary, at least by stages, to limit the money supply to the potential of production, but this is not enough. When deflation is advanced as the sole and sovereign remedy I have the nostalgic feeling that this is where I came in before. We had a great deflation and the economy did not thereafter cure itself. It was precisely at that point that I was brought in with new and dynamic measures which subsequent economists have nearly all agreed were right in the conditions of that time. At present we have an additional problem to the demand pull inflation, which can certainly be stopped by deflation though the economy must then be moved forward again by a constructive intervention of government.

The new factor is cost-push inflation caused by the inordinate power and action of some trade unions, and it can perpetuate and even exaggerate the inflation in certain vital categories even when expansion of the money supply stops. This is why the wage-price mechanism as I first called it in 1955, or prices and incomes policy as it is now called, must also be used in modern conditions. It is untrue to say that prices and incomes policy has failed; it has never yet been tried. All attempts so far have been negative, and never positive. As Mr. Len Murray put it in his able interview for The Director: "Incomes policy is too often just a matter for restraint."

The plain fact is that some have to get more and others less. The main principles of this great decision have to be settled by government elected by the whole people. Large areas of the national life covering most new enterprises should be left free of all controls. Yet in the established regions of industry someone must now settle the differentials of reward, and the only proper authority is government, after taking advice from all sides. Mistakes will be made, even after every consultation and process of reason, but not so many mistakes as in leaving everything to the anarchy of industrial conflict or the force of powerful minorities. The mind and will of elected men are more likely to reach a reasonable conclusion than the turmoil of a dogfight.

This is why in general principle we need three points of comprehension and decision: limitation of the money supply, positive action in the spheres of incomes and when necessary of prices and profits, government action to overcome the shock result of ending inflation. Would this mean trouble? We should hope not, and do everything possible to avoid it; but if there were trouble, be strong enough to meet it. It might be necessary temporarily not only to stop supplementary benefits but also to check the use of funds for strikes against arrangements settled

Last Words : Broadsheets 1970-1980

by law after verdict of the whole people at a general election. Strikes would not last long if these measures were taken and were accompanied by certain technical precautions supported by the means and the will to keep order. I led the general strike in the Midlands in 1926 and have followed the subsequent differences in science and technology; they cut both ways. What I affirm with absolute conviction is that today only will is lacking, and that this nation can be saved by the rally of a great people's will. The means are available, and I believe that their vital spirit still lives in the British people.

28

Where Is The Will To Act?

MY whole political life has rested on the belief that the present crisis would occur. It has been postponed far longer than I anticipated first by war and then by the world inflationary movement which will now aggravate the original trouble. So I will suggest remedy without pleading Bernard Shaw's excuse on the rare occasions he admitted to error — it is impossible to foresee the full extent of other people's follies.

The problem is not the impenetrable mystery sometimes indicated by economists who cannot see the wood for a recent growth of trees in a jungle of temporary expedients. Even alternative solutions have usually been available. What has always been lacking in my time is the will to act. It has often been obvious what to do, but no government dared to do it in period of peace. In terms of the basic simplicity we should always seek, the failure has been in adjusting consumption to production within a free enterprise system, without the controls of communism which stifle full production. The concomitant failure has been in organising a viable area within which the requisite action is possible. That potential first existed in the Empire, and an analogous, even greater possibility now arises in Europe.

The immediate situation can only be met by a comprehensive policy rather than by the partial measures suggested by conflicting schools of thought.

1. It is of course necessary at least by stages to limit the money supply to the potential of production. We did not need a feuding medley of variegated pundits to tell us that with redundant circumlocution. The concept was stated with

considerable clarity in Irving Fisher's work on quantity theory first published in 1911. In general it has been a commonplace of history that to increase money beyond any possibility of increasing production is bound to cause inflation.

2. Yet pure monetary theory is no longer enough, and characteristically its political protagonists emerge just as it becomes obsolete. The monopoly power of some trade unions now adds cost-push to the demand-pull inflation. The reductio ad absurdum of those who deny this is the question: would it make no difference to our production costs and competitive position if wages in some key trade unions were quadrupled? We need a statutory incomes policy which is positive as well as negative — dynamic action, not static freeze — and, after taking full advice from all available sources, the only ultimate authority must be elected government. Everyone may have to take a cut for the time being, and Ministers should give a lead by taking double the cut of anyone else.

3. The union of Europe is an economic as well as a political and inspirational necessity. How else can we insulate ourselves in any degree from the third factor of inflation imported from abroad by extremely fluctuating world prices? The answer to present difficulties is to take the foot off the brake and to accelerate toward real union. Then we can substitute great policies for small haggles: for instance the tragic paradox of ruined agriculture in Europe and starving millions in the third world. A guaranteed price over an adequate period can evoke full production from European farming, and industrial mass production for an assured market with consequent price reductions can more than offset any increase in food prices. The resultant surplus of temperate foodstuffs can be used constructively. Four years ago I urged a consortium of Europe, the Dominions and America to feed the hungry of the world from a natural surplus and to carry the cost of this great human act as a combined charge. It is clearly

now right to invite the participation of the Arabs who are the leaders of the third world* but ingenious plans to make them pay for the whole undertaking are unlikely to succeed. It is right too to ask the communist powers to join when they can; meantime the initiative may rest with Europe and America. Lift politics to a higher plane, raise the sights to further objectives, think greatly and act greatly in a manner worthy of Britain and Europe.

4. Few economists would deny it is possible to stop inflation, but it is argued that the shock to the system would be insupportable. In particular, monetary restriction would cause massive unemployment long before the power of some trade unions to demand inordinate wages was curtailed. Even if monetary policy need not be so severe because it is accompanied by the positive incomes policy here suggested, unemployment would still occur on a considerable scale unless further measures were taken. It is the fear of unemployment when inflation is stopped which paralyses government like a rabbit in front of a boa-constrictor. Therefore constructive action must be ready to deal with the consequent unemployment. This is where I came in before, as a Minister with a public works programme which was late almost universally recognised as the right remedy at that time. Yet the situation has now radically altered because the public sector is already cluttered with lame dogs in a government expenditure which must be reduced. What to do about that?

The first answer is to make the private sector viable again, so that the lame dog problem created by the errors of government will no longer arise. This means removing all price controls except in the case of monopolies, and also eliminating penal company taxation based on illusions caused by inflation. Competition will look after prices in a free enterprise society; particularly in a sphere as large as Europe where a firm will go out of business if it is less efficient than others. All we need to keep down prices is to release the creative genius of the British with fair opportunity in an area of limitless expansion potential. Monopoly is a different matter, and in such cases the cause of price rise must be controlled by government whether it be the artificial fixing of capitalist cartels or wage demands by trade unions in a position to hold the nation up to ransom. Then government must be strong, and must act.

So government can be free to do what it really should do. The business of government is not to hold the baby for a failing capitalism, whose failure it has caused itself by hand-cuffing and starving industry. The real duty of government lies in undertakings too large for private enterprise, and in encouraging the discoveries of science which can assist all enterprise. When government resources are freed from the ineffective subsidy of an impossible system, they can be used to solve creatively the unemployment problem in a sphere too large for private or municipal enterprise. It is many years since I first said that housing and similar needs of our people should be handled by the state as an operation of war. The phrase has since been used by others possessing the power of government, but nothing whatever has been done about it.

Government free from the role of meddlesome nelly can at last perform the elementary duty of any responsible man in housing our people, first promised in the "land fit for heroes to live in" of 1918. There are many other examples of appropriate and valuable action when nonsense policies belong to the past.

Government with a more serious task than preparing a budget to remove a molehill from a mountain must have a different character. It will need what I have called a different order of mind and will. Mind has often been present, but will in recent times have usually been absent. Clearly government must have power to act rapidly, but also clearly it must be entirely constitutional. This means that Parliament must be able at any time to dismiss it by vote of censure. It should be a new Parliament freshly elected to support a government drawn from the whole nation. Certainly it should contain the best of politics from all parties who are willing to face danger, and also business and trade unions should be invited, representatives of civil service and universities, and I would add defence services under the same parliamentary control as everyone else. No one except a fool seeks trouble, but government should be ready to meet it. We are faced by a crisis unparalleled in peace time which sooner or later was bound to occur. We need all that the whole nation has to offer in the union of a few years to surmount bitterness and conquer problems in a way worthy of the British genius.

29

Europe's Opponents

IF the little Englanders succeed in reducing Great Britain to an offshore island of the continent of Europe, Mr. Enoch Powell will be a most suitable Prime Minister; the diminutive surmounting a diminution. This is no reflection on his person and character which are no doubt exemplary, but is a just appreciation of the manifest absurdity of his published policies. It required no extra diligence in a small team of research workers to reveal sufficient of past follies to estimate future performances, in the unlikely event of this motley array of die-hard conservatives and obsolete socialists carrying the negative. By their fruits you shall know them, by the outcome of their policies. So this article must be given to the exposure of a negative rather than the reiteration of a European positive which has preoccupied me ever since 1946.

Take first Mr. Powell, and then his socialist colleagues, in that turgid academy of political obsolescence where all the nostrums have been tried and have failed before. "In the matter of inflation the unions are sinned against, not sinning," Mr, Powell said last night. "They are innocent as lambs, pure white as the driven snow." (*Daily Telegraph* 21.11.70). Thus encouraged from quarters indeed diverse the unions have put in claims which are now universally recognised to risk pricing Britain out of export markets. The logic of the argument was that even if wages were quadrupled it would not affect production costs: now being proved by the facts to be sheer nonsense. The contention was that cost-push inflation did not exist, only demand-pull, so a sharp deflation of the money supply was the only remedy. Here we scent the distilled essence of obsolescence, for this is exactly what was tried in the thirties by the previous monetarists. This is precisely where I was brought in before.

Every schoolboy should know from history that the printing press can wreck an economy. But economists learn from modern conditions that strong trade unions out of control can raise prices disastrously even within a rational monetary system. In the export trade they can price themselves out of a job, and in the basic services they can price other people out of employment. The fatuous fantasy continues: "There is only one way to stop Inflation" according to Mr. Powell, "and that is to float the pound". . 'Let everyone float and live happy ever after' (*Daily Telegraph* 14.6.711). We are now all floating together but the paradise of living happy ever after remains in the sky above these storm-tossed seas of increasing inflation.

"It is not true that the British can no longer defend their own country if necessary . . . nothing has altered the military importance of the North Sea and the English Channel—one of the finest anti-tank ditches in the world". (Mr. Powell, Sunday Express 5.10.69). This must mean—if it means anything—that Russian armies deployed along the Channel coast of a fallen Europe would have the same difficulty in getting across as the Germans in 1940. Mr Powell has apparently not noticed the increase of fire power in the interval which would not only render impossible the existence of any naval defence in the Channel, but could develop a curtain of fire to cover a landing capable of obliterating any defence of the beaches or their vicinity.

This trivial catalogue of wet silliness could be extended, but may halt in pity at Mr. Powell's voluntary assumption of the whole load of sins committed by the present Labour government. For he who wills the means must will the end. His boast that he put the Labour government in power may or may not be valid, but it certainly makes him responsible for what it does. No man can brag of an achievement and then disclaim its results. The logic of his vanity engulfs him in the mire of Labour's failure.

The unforeseen leap of Mr, Powell into national publicity occurred at the ripe age of 56 in the year 1968, through one foolish

Last Words : Broadsheets 1970-1980

speech about the Tiber in relation to coloured immigration; after he had languished in the relative obscurity of a 5 per cent vote for party leadership just three years previously, A member of the Establishment had broken ranks and repeated what the "certified dead" had been saying in more reasonable language ever since 1955, when it was easy to meet or rather to forestall the problem in a decent and humane fashion. As often remarked, it is noteworthy when the elephant walks on his hind legs, not that he walks well but that he should so walk at all.

The performance was applauded in the early stages by Tory interests who sought to canalise the anti-black vote, as in the thirties they had used some errant young members known as the Y.M.C.A. to attract liberal votes, and later was well advertised by the astute managers of Labour in the hope of splitting the Conservative party. It evoked a more academic interest from Lord Hailsham: "I feared the irrational in human nature even in the balmy days when Mr. Powell, Minister of Health, was busy importing West Indian nurses to manage his hospitals." (The Spectator 19 7 69). It appears that these vacancies had occurred in 1962 after nurses and mid wives had asked an increase of salaries from 20 to 25 per cent, while Mr Powell's department only granted them an increase of two-and-a-half per cent.

At first sight this does not appear a very sound foundation for a coalition with Messrs. Foot and Benn in yet another negative, this time to the hopes of Europe. Yet as Lord Chatham observed in his simile of the union of the rivers Rhone and Saone near Lyon: "different as they are they meet at last". My initial feelings for Michael Foot and Wedgwood Benn are infused with atavistic warmth, for their respective fathers were two of the finest characters in the older generation when I was the youngest MP. It is indeed sad to see the vital stream of that sturdy radicalism lost in the arid sands of British bureaucracy and European negation. Isaac Foot, though an eminent authority on Cromwell, was always available for all human causes in opposition to the dead and repressive hand, while the original Wedgwood Benn with his outstanding record in the First World War was always ardent in European reconciliation and advancement.

Why then retreat into the empty shell of dead forms? Why deny modern Europe in the name of 19th century British socialism? Why hold the baby for capitalism by taking over obsolete industries at the already overburdened public expense, instead of giving leadership over the whole field of industry by an incomes policy which is positive as well as negative? Miners, doctors, nurses, scientists, should have had more long ago, and others should have less, but this requires the dynamic and persistent intervention of government to replace the destructive anarchy of powerful interests. Prices will certainly be kept down by full European competition in which only the efficient will survive, but British industry must first be free from penal taxation and the stifling grip of bureaucratic control. Above all, in present circumstances, the weed undergrowth of local authority waste must be cut right back by central authority. In short, Britain must be made fit for a greater future by "the pervading influence of a commanding administration." The quotation has been lifted with only one word altered from beneath the primrose wreath to assuage any outrage of the old conservatism at the suggestion of effective action by modern government.

The part of government is to do things too big for private enterprise by backing our brilliant science up to the hilt as the hope of a future which new discoveries can at any time revolutionise, and by undertakings beyond the range of local authority such as the rehousing of our people like an operation of war. Thus it can create the conditions in which private enterprise can succeed. What a parody of government to make it a collector of lame ducks, while a bankrupt island lives on external charity in the hope that world trade may one day turn up. Even the much discussed deficit with Europe, regarded in basic economic terms, is part of our subsidy. How long will they continue to send us goods for nothing? The answer is only so long as it suits them in the mad scramble of small, competitive countries all to achieve simultaneously a favourable balance of payments, in default of European economic and monetary union. If Europe becomes a going concern without us, our trade whether in deficit or surplus can be excluded any day at their convenience. If we are inside we can put our house in order to achieve a fair balance, and none can deny us our success.

Meantime the cause of Europe proceeds to oratorial music which Bernard Shaw would again have described as the funeral march of a fried eel. The jingle of the pence drowns all appeal to larger considerations and further objectives. The triviality of the discussion establishes a new record in the mean and mediocre against a background of vast danger but yet of bright opportunity. Where is the sense even of homecoming in reunion with the lands of nearly all our origins? Where is the deep relief that the flower of European youth can never again be thrown to mutual murder by a system which has failed? Where is the passion for Europe felt in the knowledge of a sublime culture inherited from three millennia of great history, and inspired by vision of the ultimate heights we can reach together? These things will live tomorrow beyond the dust of today.

30

Alternative Policy and Will

IT is no longer necessary to argue that the state of Britain is serious: this is now recognised. The question is what method and policy become necessary. The present method is an alternation between two parties which have been in power since the first war. At the end of that conflict in which Britain had nearly double the casualties of the second war we were still the greatest power in the world. Since then government has been exercised about two-thirds of the time by the Conservative Party and one-third by the Labour Party with results now clear in the contrast of our present situation. The brief coalition of the parties in the thirties not only continued but in long effect accentuated the decline. The hope therefore appears illusory that change of party or coalition can provide the necessary method. The shrewd latent instinct of the British people may soon adapt for its own purpose a decisive, observation: politics have become too serious to be left only to the politicians.

We need agreement that the situation is at least as serious as wartime, in some ways more acute because union and action are more difficult to secure in the absence of an obvious external enemy. Government therefore requires for a period the same concentration of national resources as in wartime and an even greater degree of will. Britain deserves the best the whole country has to offer. None should be excluded, certainly not politicians among whom are some excellent and experienced men and women. The point is simply that alone they are not enough. Their rule would have brought bankruptcy already except for the discovery and financial prospect of North Sea oil, which can be a large factor in recovery if glut evoked by the present price level and the American effort at self-sufficiency do not produce price collapse.

Last Words : Broadsheets 1970-1980

This is the second time science has saved the nation from the errors of politics. As Sir Winston Churchill frequently observed, Russian armies would have overrun Europe and the position of Britain would have become impossible but for the discovery of nuclear fission by the scientists, which no-one could have foreseen when the policies leading to this situation were initiated. The fact that we would be dead on two counts already but for the unforeseen and unforeseeable intervention of science, combined with the contrast between Britain's position in 1918 and the present, provides a simple answer to the question: are the parties enough? Clearly we need also the best to be offered by science, business, trade unions, civil service, universities and fighting services.

Can anything less than such an impulse of national resolution produce the will to do even the obvious? The results must be faced of maintaining the money supply at a level no higher than the potential of production; reducing public expenditure to the means of the country with all the scrapping of favourite plans, obsolete and irrelevant ideologies which this entails; revising the whole system of taxation which kills initiative, and at least equating our incentives to brains and energy with that of our European partners; making incomes policy positive as well as negative by paying the rate for the job on merit and relating it directly to production; meeting unemployment constructively after dealing with inflation: these needs are clear, but demand a degree of will in government now lacking.

When we pass beyond the self-evident requirements of the emergency, government for a period should be pragmatic rather than ideological. Office always reveals fresh difficulties but also fresh opportunities which can be realised by will in government with the aid of a civil service which can still be a superb instrument of action. In the menacing and rapidly changing modern situation of infinite complexity it is as idle to pretend that Parliament can control every detail as to contend that shareholders should sit in the boardroom discussing, delaying and instructing managing

Alternative Policy and Will

directors in every decision of daily business. Yet it is quite possible to combine the necessary system of effective action with the complete maintenance of our democratic constitution and the full control of elected Parliament. The abuse of power can be prevented and individual liberty scrupulously preserved by the ability of Parliament to dismiss government at any time with vote of censure.

The concept that any government would or could cling to power after such a verdict in a developed country is a complete illusion. The people have the simple remedy of staying at home until the government falls, and this would soon happen. It is axiomatic that the general strike in an advanced country would defeat any government which has not the support of the people. It is equally true that a freshly elected government with the full approval of the country behind it can meet and overcome any challenge. No government of the kind here described should accept power without the mandate of a General Election.

No-one in his senses seeks confrontation, but in the event of sad necessity it should be firmly met. The idea is more than obsolete; the tradition becomes dangerous and destructive that rewards can only be settled by the dog-fight of the market place in which the heavyweights of the large organisations must always win irrespective of any man's contribution to production or the national well-being. In this vital sphere of the modern world elected government alone must govern. Certainly it should continually consult trade unions together with every other valuable organ of national life, and should delegate detail after determining main principles. But a challenge to government's ultimate authority can and should be met by a simple paralysis of all funds involved until the challenge is over.

When this essential principle of elected government's authority is recognised, trade unions would discover not a lesser but a larger role in the life of the modern state. Fascinating possibilities of syndicalism in industries already nationalised and workers'

Last Words : Broadsheets 1970-1980

participation safeguarded by confidence agreements in much of private enterprise, could now enter serious consideration and engage the experience and constructive energies of trade union leaders. Again the approach should be pragmatic in careful experiments. In this sphere I affirm only my long held view that the part of the State is to be pioneer in alliance with science rather than a nurse holding the baby for failing industries. Once stifling taxation and oppressive regulations are lifted from the back of industry, the role of the State is to create the conditions in which private enterprise can operate and to assist science to open up new opportunities for its development.

It should not be beyond the wit of man to equate production and consumption in a viable area where executive government can effectively control its own affairs. Britain has now taken the first step in entering Europe, but instead of expediting complete union to reap the benefit authority is adopting a slight deflation while waiting for world trade to turn up and enable all nations to achieve the international dream of selling simultaneously more than they buy. British experience over years has certainly proved that anyone can either deflate or inflate. It remains to be shown that government with adequate access to raw materials - possible for Europe by special arrangements with British Dominions or African countries - and control over its own market, can enable the people to consume full production in a stable price level.

This means the evolution of continental systems within which the main human experiments — American capitalism, the two versions of communism in Russia and China, the third method of government leading free enterprise which should be developed in Europe, can eventually prove peacefully which system is the best. Instead of interfering in each other's affairs and violating the principle of Helsinki, the idea may gradually occur within nuclear paralysis that the most effective persuasion of mankind is to show what works well; the ultimate hope is even to learn something from each other. All this of course can be considered a departure from reality by existing authority, which thus dismisses any attempt to surpass the failure of today in a way the people may accept tomorrow when the results of present policies are strikingly reflected in their daily lives.

Strong government is certainly needed to insist on adequate armaments until some measure of universal disarmament can be attained and reason can prevail, also to maintain internal order during the difficulties of transition from near collapse to new equilibrium and progress. Four years can and must be sufficient for such a government, because Britain awake never allows much longer to executive men, although our people sometimes indulge a Walpole for protracted periods of slumber.

Temporary measures of rigour may be necessary at home touching life and industry at no more points than really necessary, and always rigidly maintaining the vital principle of individual liberty before the law. We may have to seek temporary favours from our European partners such as selective protection of certain industries until full industrial health is restored. They will be more readily granted to a British government which is truly European and can give credible guarantees at the end of the specified period to enter a full European union with due warning to our industries to get ready for that testing event. We need the ability both to persuade and to act at home and abroad. I believe that in crisis deeply felt the vital qualities can still be found in the British people.

31

Crisis and Straw-Clutching Policies

AFTER much time and emotion spent on change which is no change it may be well to consider changes which can soon become necessary to the life of the nation. All parties now accept in varying degree the conduct of business by the State. My premise is that the business of the State is to make possible private enterprise. For this purpose government should intervene only at the key points of the modern situation. Where monopoly exists, either capitalist or trade union, it is the duty of government to prevent the community being held to ransom. In such event creative enterprise cannot function. Where conditions of free competition prevail prices and profits can look after themselves, and so best serve the general economy through incentive to maximal production. Yet this is clearly not the case when a capitalist monopoly controls the market, or a trade union in reality controls a nationalised industry and can insist both on an exorbitant wage and on the maintenance of redundancy for its labour. It is therefore idle in present conditions to speak either of the free market or of the social justice of socialism. The problem must be faced with fresh minds and clear eyes.

The argument between monetary and incomes policy becomes in these circumstances largely irrelevant. It is clear that both are required in more profound and strenuous application than has yet been contemplated. It is certain that inflation will occur if the money supply is not limited at least to the potential of production, and it is equally clear that the monopoly position of some trade unions will then secure a still more disproportionate share of the limited supply if government does not intervene. To maintain and enhance the differential rewards which at all levels

Crisis and Straw-Clutching Policies

are the incentives to efficiency, it is evident that government action must be positive and not negative. A frozen posture is no answer to a dynamic situation.

A solution to these problems requires first an answer to the question - who governs? It is an answer which both parties in the high test of office have failed to supply. Their conduct has been to inflate and to spend until the bubble burst. Their only subsequent move has been to apply the deflation of the thirties with consequent unemployment, a policy now identical to both parties with only difference of degree between them. Also revived is the old hope of that period for an "export led" recovery by a drive into world markets, which means in practice exporting unemployment as each nation tries simultaneously to sell more than it buys with such devices as competitive devaluations. We are back to square one. There we shall remain until some government combines the limitation of the money supply with a positive incomes policy relating reward directly to production, and eliminates both internal and external deficits with a severity beyond the concept of present politics. In a situation presenting a danger equivalent to wartime we may temporarily require something approaching a siege economy, until we are fit again to take our full part in a completed European community with a viable economy capable of equating production with consumption on a continental scale and enjoying a wide choice of overseas connections with raw material supplies.

Faced with such problems and possible necessities can any serious analysis lead to the conclusion that party government will be adequate? Equally illusory is the hope that in coalition a combination of policies and personnel responsible for the present situation can succeed. No more time should be lost in clutching the straws of fluctuating statistics. A national government drawn from the whole country alone can meet a crisis which in our case is not only cyclical but also fundamental. Some from the parties can certainly provide the valuable factor of experience in an administrative machine which must be greatly changed, but new minds from a far wider range of life's tests will be required and above all an executive will power recently lacking.

Would then the firm principle that government alone governs inevitably produce confrontation with trade union or other interests? That depends largely on the gravity of the situation and on the clarity with which government explains it. If a challenge to national survival arises our people can still be capable of a great response. In this crisis of peacetime the will to survive can be freely expressed in a freshly elected Parliament. Democracy would be scrupulously preserved in every particular by the power of Parliament to dismiss government at any time by a vote of censure. But subject to this safeguard government should ask Parliament to confer on it the ability of rapid action. Main questions could often be remitted with advantage to referenda for the verdict of the people which government should accept even after a statement of their view had been rejected.

Executive government can always find more than one way of doing what has to be done, and resignation should only follow complete frustration. Experience of office teaches all concerned that preconceptions often prove impractical, but at the same time new prospects open and other means can be found to do what is needed with the aid of a Civil Service still superb in the hard core and ever ready to assist a government of clear mind and real will.

Confrontation between trade unions and a government subject to a freshly elected Parliament and sustained by frequent referenda becomes less likely, particularly if trade unions together with employers' organisation and every other relevant interest are constantly consulted in the formation of policy. If any challenge to the authority of elected government arises it must be resolutely met. This is easier now in the decisive sphere of public opinion because government can talk face to face with everyone on television and radio. One evening can be as effective in persuasion as years of the largest public meetings ever held in

Crisis and Straw-Clutching Policies

previous experience. Capable ministers would also invite to this confrontation not of force but of democracy, trade union leaders and other notables who were opposed to their policies. Men who are incapable of sustaining their position in such debate are unfit, unworthy of their office and the public trust. They would either prevail or make way for better men. Are we really then to believe that government resting on a newly elected Parliament and supported by frequent referenda, ready to consult trade unions at any time in private or to meet them in public debate, would be subject to any interest other than the will of the whole people? If a general strike is called the weight of public opinion with consequent popular action would be decisive. Serious precaution by government supported by the will of the neighbourhood would keep the key services going and maintain the life of the nation.

Once the question - who governs? - is settled by one way or the other in favour of government elected by majority vote, new possibilities of opportunity and achievement will open to trade unions and other vital essences of national life. Participation to evoke the partnership of the worker at the point which really interests him - increasing his production and therefore his wage - is an invitation to close co-operation between government, industrialists and trade unions: participation too in the development of the Welfare State on lines both more economic and more popular because people would contribute only to get what they want: participation in careful experiments of worker-ownership in industries already nationalised with reversion to private enterprise if this fails after fair trial. Government, trade unions and employers' organisations would be partners in great adventures. Some hopes would be frustrated and should therefore be quickly abandoned by firm and rapid decision, but our beckoning science continually opens new vistas of ever greater development for a dynamic partnership between government and industry. Survival and progress become a matter of will in a great people: "the world is character".

32

The Need For A Contingency Plan

TWO clear views of the present situation appear now to emerge from many complexities. Our economy will soon be floated off the rocks by North Sea oil. Until then we can borrow enough to keep going while the trade unions are induced by monetary restriction to accept wage restraint and the necessary economies are made in public expenditure. There may be a risk that competitors with lower production costs in any temporary oil glut can put us out of business, but they could always be persuaded to be reasonable. In contrary opinion the crisis is not superficial but fundamental and has been building up over long years. We are non-competitive in a large range of industries whose exports must pay for our imports of food and raw materials; even oil at best will not bridge the ultimate deficit. A surgical operation is necessary to make our economy viable again, and this can include over a period of time a siege economy.

My whole political life has rested on the latter belief which is now shared by an increasing number of people. This view is particularly evident abroad and is reflected increasingly in our exchange rate. However I still do not find the least difficulty in meeting the tactfully deployed continental surmise that our country is now decadent. The reply is that we are all very different people when asleep to when we are awake. Most of British history could be written in terms of Britain awake or Britain asleep. Our country is at present asleep and as usual will require different policies, different leadership, in short a different order of mind and will when it again awakens.

The view of deep crisis was naturally rejected by a majority of our countrymen while things still went relatively smoothly. It

The Need For A Contingency Plan

is a nearly whole-time job to appraise all the facts by reading journals and books in several languages and meeting specialists in various countries. This process is not available to most people who consequently recognise facts only when they are hit by them. No great people are roused to great action until it is plainly necessary. It is my confident belief that the British will then prove themselves greater than ever within Europe. Meantime we need a contingency plan in case things get worse, which should now be the subject of constant consideration and discussion among those sufficiently informed to feel that the disaster can occur even if they think it is improbable.

Many minds now move in the direction of winning time to put our house in order. The question of import controls in addition to a floating exchange rate naturally arises at this point. The basic dilemma is that when such policies are made really effective they can evoke a worse disaster by incurring our exclusion from foreign and even from European markets. The world does not owe us a living not even Europe, and we have already tried the patience of the Common Market by our initial tardiness and by later playing the brake on the wheel to most forward projects.

We need to lift our policies into a totally different context to gain European consent for a period of siege economy to make our industries viable again. Certainly it may be necessary to exclude many imports from our home market while we are non-competitive, particularly while we experiment with new methods to become competitive again. Suggestions to spread unemployment by shorter hours, or preferably by shift systems to run machines throughout the 24 hours, should not only be examined but operated in careful experiment. The result of modernisation with British technical ingenuity can again put us in the lead. The intense interest of the task can produce a new understanding between trade unions and perceptive government which could and should provide differentials with real incentive to skill and production at every level. But the period of trial and error at home can render us particularly vulnerable abroad. We

Last Words : Broadsheets 1970-1980

have still to sell enough on other markets to live while avoiding the disruption of our delicate home market by their customary competition.

This basic dilemma can be overcome not by retreat into an island fortress which starves without foreign markets but by becoming at last truly European. We should take our foot off the brake and put it hard on the accelerator, but first ask time to make our engine work. We should say to fellow Europeans that at the end of four years - or possibly sooner we will be ready for a common European currency with an end to balance of payments problems within the continent, and a measure of common government. First however they must bear with us while we make ourselves fairly competitive in these conditions. A British government which was convincingly European could win time for the necessary period of recuperation if it were certain to be followed by a system which all true Europeans desire; three clearly defined spheres between European, national and regional government. How many problems could then fall into place; even we English might benefit from the general devolution. Many will feel that such suggestions go too far, are a contrast to current confusion which is too fantastic, but some will at least agree that all contingency plans should be discussed in a sombre situation of gathering gravity.

After long and bitter experience we can all surely agree that democracy should be entirely preserved. Yet like everything else in modern conditions procedure needs to be modernised. For any great achievement a freshly elected Parliament is necessary. That Parliament should have the ability any day to dismiss government by vote of censure. Is not this the essence of democracy? If this power is scrupulously preserved time could be saved and effective action secured by creating much the same relationship between Parliament and government as between shareholders and a board of directors. Every abuse could be ventilated, and failure or misuse of power would incur dismissal. This was the original power and procedure of Parliament. While

The Need For A Contingency Plan

we advance we can regard the first purpose and retain the right then won and later developed. Government must be strong but not a tyrant.

The light of experience can illumine all plans with a clear recollection for those who have been in government. Facts learnt in government can not only modify previous opinions but can open new prospects. It was not until I had lived for nearly a year in a room at the Treasury that I was able to propose plans which were subsequently accorded an approval denied them at the time. The enduring lesson was that many preconceptions are corrected but many new opportunities are revealed. What matters are open eyes and a persisting dynamism? We can only take into government with certainty some clear guiding principles.

Real government should rest on leadership rather than compulsion. Certainly in time of crisis a government would have the necessary authority if it were drawn from the whole nation and sustained by a freshly elected Parliament. It should include without fear or favour all from past or present who have something essential to contribute, and should exclude none on grounds of prejudice or passion. The administration should have emergency powers of action but should use them only when necessary, and in such situations should never interfere with what is working well. The task is to repair not to disrupt, and for this purpose all should be consulted but the word of elected government alone should be final. Progress at last should be combined with order, because without order there can be no enduring progress, and without progress there can be no stable order. At the end of four years a government of this character should make way for the return of more normal conditions, because our sensible British people never put up with really executive men for much longer than they are necessary, while in any case their task would be done. Their reward would be the renaissance of a great country.

33

New Men and New Policies

THE business of government is to make possible private enterprise, not to conduct business. This view differs sharply both from the socialism which buys up unworkable industries at the public expense and from the monetarism which believes that a limitation of the money supply can solve all our problems. The deflation of the thirties appears now to be the policy of both parties, accompanied only by the remnants of an entirely negative incomes policy. The result is increasing unemployment, and the elimination of differential rewards for skill. Such a system cannot last.

All this is a crude reaction from the follies of inflation which were well understood even before Keynes, who is now absurdly reputed not to have realised that an increase of the money supply beyond any hope of increasing production causes soaring prices. That the money supply must at least be limited to the potential of production is an elementary fact recently ignored. The modern question is how to provide an assured market for full production, and how to evoke it by differential reward for skill and effort.

A limitation of the money supply to the possibility of production must be accompanied by an incomes policy which is positive as well as negative. Otherwise a still more disproportionate share of the limited purchasing power is grabbed by the big battalions of unskilled labour with trade union strength. All differential rewards for skill-whether toolmakers in the factory or the highest managerial ability in administration are gradually, or rapidly squeezed out. The free market of the monetarists' dream no longer exists. Both trade union power and capitalist monopoly have brought it to an end.

New Men and New Policies

This is why government must either intervene or abdicate to anarchy. Skill which is unprotected by the big battalions must be the special charge of government, in particular the life of the nation depends on the scientists who in one generation have saved Europe from conquest and this island from bankruptcy by the discovery of nuclear fission and North Sea oil. Laissez-faire is as obsolete as nationalisation. An entirely new principle is required in government: making private enterprise possible by protecting what makes it work.

Changes of this magnitude can only be implemented by a government drawn from the whole nation, business as well as politics, some trade unionists as well as some from the fighting services in a period of danger. A freshly elected Parliament is essential to provide such a government with the requisite moral authority and to secure the full principle of democracy by the ability to dismiss it any day with vote of censure. Present inhibitions would thereby be overcome. No-one in his senses seeks confrontation, but any government of mind and will must be ready to meet it.

A strike called against such a government supported by a freshly elected Parliament would have no chance of success, because it would lack the necessary public support. The paralysis of all strike funds proposed by Lloyd George's government to meet the threat of the Triple Alliance in 1919 would be more than adequate. The abhorrent principle of special powers to imprison, then suggested by some members of that government, would not only be wrong but quite unnecessary to a competent modern government. Those who were threatening the life of the country by withholding vital services against the declared will of the nation should be named, and invited on to television to defend themselves in debate with competent members of the government. The resultant social pressure of their fellows would be more than sufficient to end the nonsense.

Vigorous and creative government could and should establish

Last Words : Broadsheets 1970-1980

quite different relations with trade unions in a crisis economy. The leaders should again be invited, initially through the powerful means of television, to co-operate with government in saving the country by new methods. A crisis economy might temporarily involve the exclusion of unnecessary imports while industry experimented with the running of machines through the 24 hours in a shift system, and other possibilities of eliminating unemployment which would be particularly attractive to trade union members. In such a crisis we could no longer be bound by the international illusion which ruined even the genius of the Keynesian conception. It will at length be realised that this country cannot indefinitely sell nearly a third of its total production on world markets which are increasingly subject to artificial undercutting and Russian dumping to break world capitalism, and that the relatively small European countries cannot all simultaneously sell more than they buy.

We cannot retreat into an island fortress after the loss of the Empire which alone made possible a national policy by assured access to food and raw materials. On the other hand in common with several European countries we need a few years of crisis economy to squeeze the wind and water out of national life before we are ready for the full operation of an European economy with the necessary surplus to develop any overseas sources of supply which may still be necessary from our own Dominions or elsewhere. We should prepare in this period with foreign policy to replace international chaos by the evolution of a series of continental systems with self-contained sources of supply and markets.

Government stuck fast in the mud of small failures must be lifted to large objectives. An example is the debate on devolution which now threatens the breakup of the United Kingdom. Yet this problem which affects all Europe today may be made the basis of a European future. European local regional patriotisms are very strong. At that level people rightly want to run their own affairs according to their diverse traditions. This presently disruptive force in a higher synthesis can be used for creative purposes. Clearly defined functions for three-tier government, regional, national and European can be the future of our continent.

In a policy of first things first, the main consideration at present is the survival of Europe. If we so disarm that we are a sitting duck, the temptation to take us over may become irresistible. We must remain at least equally armed without any cuts unless and until adequate inspection can make sure they are mutual. In these conditions the Marxist mind says "why climb a tall tree and risk a broken neck when you can sit underneath it and wait for the apples to fall into your hands?", and at present the western world is providing plenty of evidence in support of this view. Parity in arms combined with constructive economic achievement in Europe can change the psychology of mankind. World stability can be strangely maintained by the terrible deterrent power of modern science. Five different continental systems in America, Europe, Russia, China and possibly in the Far East around Japan could then in the fair competition of compulsory peace prove which is the best. When we can no longer fight each other, we may even learn something from each other.

34

Mosley Debates with the Irish Prime Minister

MOSLEY debated with the Irish Prime Minister at the Law Students' Debating Society, Dublin, on November 2.1978. The motion was "That so far Western Democracy has failed". We print below an abbreviated text of his speech which was unreported in the British press.

Mosley said: It was necessary to define democracy. Should it not be the system which implemented the expressed will of the people? It has so far failed for discernible reasons. The question was how to make this best system work. The first answer was to modernise Parliamentary procedure. The relationship of Parliament to Government should be more like that of shareholders to a board of directors. The essence of democracy could be preserved if Parliament could dismiss government at any time by vote of censure, and have the right always to interrogate Ministers on such questions as human rights.

The Main Question of the Age

Democracy had so far failed to meet the main question of the age, which was to equate production and consumption, to enable the people to consume what they could produce. When science had solved the problem of production it was a tragedy to have millions unemployed in the Western world while unnecessary poverty and suffering existed for lack of the goods they could produce. The first reason for this failure was the absence of a viable area with a reliable market. All governments were at the mercy of world chaos as they all tried to sell abroad more than they bought. Britain only kept going by the chance discoveries of science such as North Sea oil, and by playing small tricks with the exchanges. He suggested a viable area free from the chaos of world markets within which government could act effectively. This action should be to make possible private enterprise. Both the nationalisation of the old socialism and the laissez-faire of the old capitalism were obsolete. Government should have an incomes policy which is positive as well as negative. Otherwise all differentials – all reward to particular skill – disappeared under pressure of the big battalions of the relatively unskilled. Government should prevent exploitation by monopoly whether trade union or capitalist. All reward should be related to production. Government should only intervene at these key points. Europe could provide the viable area with a self-contained market and access to necessary raw materials and some extra foodstuffs. Foreign policy should seek the emergence of five continental systems each with a greater productive potential than the whole world possessed a few years ago. There could be a European system, an American system, two different systems of communism in Russia and China, and a fifth system in the Far East round Japan. Let the future be decided by proving which was the best. A world thus organised would have nothing to fight about. But they should not disarm until they were satisfied it was mutual. When this was done the systems might even learn something from each other.

European Structure

In our European system he suggested a three-tier government - regional, national and European - in three clearly defined spheres. Throughout Europe there was strong regional feeling which now threatened the disruption of existing states. Yet devolution of many of the duties of government to the regions could turn this danger to an advantage, and provide the basis of the future European system. In Britain there should be at least two regions in England as well as Scotland and Wales. They would be linked at the national level. European government should certainly be charged with defence and if possible with the preservation of human rights in the various regions. Regional suspicions and animosities could thus be overcome. It was for them to think about their Irish problem in terms of regional solutions within a European system.

The Immigration Question

The possibilities of a European system were endless. The purchasing power of a united Europe in raw materials could open many political doors. Some 12 million immigrants in Europe would want to go home as the European crisis developed. But their home lands were at present closed against them and these doors could only be opened by the economic power of a united Europe. This was the only possible solution to the immigration problem.

The Balance of the World

In a greater sphere the policy of a truly united Europe could hold the balance of the world. There was a danger in the present division of world power between America and Russia. It was necessary to make Europe great again. We are all small nations now but within Europe could each again wield a great influence. The wisdom of Irish statesmanship for example could make the same contribution to the future peace of Europe as the energy and courage of Irish soldiers had made to the European wars of the past.

The Rebirth of Europe

The history of our peoples had been interwoven for centuries, from the days of classic Greece and Rome. We now needed to turn that sentiment into a practical fact. As present policies failed to work it would be realised that great things could be done in a great way. The renaissance of Europe should at present be developed as a great contingency plan. In an age of cynical disillusionment men required a new inspiration. Here was the cause to inspire - the rebirth of Europe.

35

United Europe Alone Can Solve the Immigration Problem

SIR OSWALD MOSLEY in 1954 asked that all immigration into our crowded island should be stopped. If his advice had been accepted the present problem would never have arisen. In 1959 he fought an election on this issue but the country was not yet aware of it. Now it is too late for any limitation of free entry to do more than touch the fringe of the question. It is the multiplication of those already here which creates a problem that cannot be solved without repatriation.

Many immigrants now here want to leave, and many more will in the coming economic crisis. The difficulty is that their countries of origin are generally unwilling to receive them. The basic facts would not be altered by the payment of a bonus Britain cannot afford which at the end of a short spending spree would merely result in larger unemployment queues in these depressed countries. Mosley suggests on the contrary a constructive policy; that these doors can only be opened by the economic power of a united Europe. Bulk purchase of raw materials and some foodstuffs on a European scale would offer to some countries an overwhelming inducement to resettle immigrants in extensive and prosperous employment, and to other countries the offer of European technology would be equally persuasive. European policy alone can be effective, for the economic power of our reduced island is clearly inadequate. Nothing is more ridiculous or repugnant than nationalist policies which propose to put nearly 2,000,000 people into ships — including women and children screaming dissent in face of mankind — for transport to countries which will not receive them. Such policies are entirely bogus.

Last Words : Broadsheets 1970-1980

In reality there are only two choices. The first is to leave existing immigrants in our overcrowded island, with the inevitable result that the present situation will in time be accentuated by natural process. The second is to take the lead in a European policy which solves a problem common to all Europe, but this policy is only available to Europeans. Mosley has been as consistent in proposing the true union of Europe as in opposing immigration, which was originally open to the 950,000,000 inhabitants of the old Empire. Mosley Secretariat now invites our readers to consider who is likely to be right in present and future in the light of who has been right in the past. The following quotations may assist judgment :-

Mosley 22.11.54: "The remedy was to give the coloured people good conditions in their own homelands. They would then be only too glad to go back... They were the victims of people who brought them here to exploit them. It was the exploiter, not the victim, he was after."

Mosley 7.4.56: "I have never had any quarrel with the coloured people. I have said they are getting a raw deal, and we should give them employment in their own countries instead of them having to come here ... Africa will be used to provide all the raw materials that Europe needs."

Mosley 19.9.58: "The sugar industry of Jamaica should be restored by action of British government as it was previously ruined ... The immigrants are the victims ... they should be returned immediately to their homelands ... there should be no violence against them ... no trace of bullying or hostility. Those who are criminal among them should be treated by rigorous enforcement of the ordinary criminal law."

The National Executive of the Labour Party 29.9.58 stated it strongly opposed any "legislation limiting Commonwealth immigration into this country."

United Europe Alone Can Solve the Immigration Problem

Mr. R. A. Butler, Conservative Home Secretary, 7.9.58 emphasised the right of coloured people "to come in and out of the Mother Country at will."

Mr. R. A. Butler 17.8.72: "We didn't dream it would end like this."

Mr. Powell 11.10.64: "I have set and always will set my face like flint against making any difference between one citizen and another on grounds of his origin."

Mr. Powell 22.4.68: "Like the Roman, I seem to see the River Tiber foaming with much blood."

Lord Hailsham 19.7.69: "I feared the irrational in human nature even in the balmy days when Mr. Enoch Powell, Minister of Health, was busy importing West Indians into his hospitals."

Mr. Winston Churchill M.P. 23.1.77: "Far from warning of the dangers of large-scale immigration into Britain at a time when the problem could have been avoided, Mr. Powell was part of the political generation responsible for that immigration. As Minister of Health he had presided over a government department that positively encouraged immigrants to come."

Law and Order

Mosley at every stage has offered constructive and humane solutions to the problem. The maintenance of opposite policies by all the parties now threatens law and order, the stability of the state. Again Mosley policy has been clear and consistent over long years. The police are a priority; they should be well paid and treated and consequently brought up to full strength. This is necessary not only to prevent ever-increasing crime but also to preserve free speech, the basis of democracy without which it really does not exist. For years past free speech in Britain has been denied to Mosley. The large halls where he continued after the

Last Words : Broadsheets 1970-1980

war to draw audiences, record in size, and orderly, were refused by local Labour majorities, while Conservative governments banned his open air demonstrations at any suggestion of hostile action. Television was also denied him until the publication of his book *My Life* in 1968 when he was allowed to appear on Panorama and drew a 9,000,000 audience; subsequently he was more normally treated.

Television has now rendered obsolete all previous propaganda methods and should be available to all who are proved to draw large audiences. Public interest, not private prejudice, should decide. All halls in the country should be available to all on payment of the normal fee. A reinforced police force alone should be charged with the maintenance of order and free speech. Any violation of this basis of the democratic state should in law be subject to severe penalties. Mosley's "private army" which was the subject of special legislation restored law and order and free speech when they had previously ceased to exist, but such individual action should neither be necessary nor allowed under any serious government which was itself prepared to keep order.

If halls and television were fairly available to all who can draw audiences the closure of streets to the general public by demonstration and mob action would no longer be necessary to free speech, and should no longer be allowed. The rights of minorities should not prevent the right of the majority to go about their normal business in peace and safety. In short, law and order, democracy and free speech depend on firm government, which for a period should be drawn not only from the parties but from the whole nation with the support of the people proved by the essential test of a general election.

36

National Government and the Confusion of Parties

IS party warfare of the old kind enough to meet the present situation, or do we need a national government drawn from the whole country to face dangers as grave as wartime? Let us first be clear what is meant by such a government. It is not a coalition of old parties which have failed already. It is not any form of dictatorship which sets aside democracy. It is government for four years during the lifetime of a freshly elected parliament, after which the old parties can return or new parties arise in a period again normal.

The question is whether anything of the kind is necessary? The politicians reply no, and some of the ablest among them argue that government should do less, not more. They are right in suggesting that an inflated bureaucracy now piles rules and regulations on people and industry which stifle initiative and waste time. They are wrong in not realising we are up against a crisis requiring major decisions in a changed world which can only come from a new government with the authority of a truly national majority behind it.

Certainly the best of politics should not be excluded. They have done their best, but their best is not good enough. Such a government should also include for its limited period the best of business, trade unions, science which alone can find answers to many problems of this age, and the fighting services who have life-long training in facing danger. Those who are free to participate in politics should meet frequently to have ready a contingency plan if and when a great crisis arises. They should be ready then to put up candidates in every constituency at a

Last Words : Broadsheets 1970-1980

general election. If among them are some competent in television debate this decisive medium would be sufficient to defeat party machines already baffled by the present size of the electorate and discredited by failure. This majority in the House of Commons would confer on government the power of rapid action as in wartime, subject always to the strict preservation of democracy by the right of parliament to dismiss government at any time with a vote of censure and always to interrogate ministers on such questions as human rights.

Is all this necessary? Can Britain just keep going as we are? The parties were only saved before from economic crisis by armament boom and the Second World War, and have since been sustained by world inflation which postponed but ultimately made worse industrial crisis. We lost our Empire owing to the war and we now face intensive competition on world markets. The old system is gone and we need a new one.

The answer is a European system within which we face only fair competition for our industries and in politics can become a great power again. But this means making Europe a reality with three-tier government in clearly defined spheres, regional, national and European. So far from impairing our national character it is the only way to save it from destruction in a world of great powers. The economic strength of all Europe can be great enough not only to provide us with a stable market but also by the joint purchase of raw materials and extra food to make good bargains with African and other countries. For instance they would then accept our immigrants who desire to return through doors now closed. As a small island we are no longer large enough, and would incur disastrous retaliation on world markets if we attempted to protect our industries. Europe alone is great enough in economics to build a new system and in politics to hold the balance of the world.

Such a continental system is a viable area within which government can solve the main economic problem of the age by equating production and consumption. The people must be able to consume their own full production, in freedom from unemployment and poverty, the monstrous spectacle of men and machines idle while so many lack the goods they could produce. No government can even begin the task while it is dependent on the chaos of world markets with all the diverse and ever-changing conditions of the globe. Effective government needs an area where it can intervene when necessary in key questions such as wages and prices, not to conduct industry but to make possible private enterprise.

The answer is neither the laissez-faire to which all parties now return nor the nationalisation which has been proved a failure in the conduct of industry by the state. What is called incomes policy has not worked well because as usual it is entirely negative without any element of the positive. It is not only necessary to limit the gains of the big trade union battalions of the unskilled but also to secure the differentials of the skilled who will gradually cease to exist without the incentive of just rewards. As I pointed out long ago in first proposing the "wage-price mechanism" the open market has disappeared over large areas in face of both capitalist and trade union monopoly.

Necessary limitation of the money supply to prevent inflation can result in an even more disproportionate share of disposable income being seized by the economic power of the trade unions of the unskilled and the differential rewards of the skilled being further reduced. Where free competition prevails any price control is unnecessary. But state protection of essential services is always necessary, whether they be police, fighting services or the skilled without trade union power. To refuse such protection is the abdication of government. We need strength in national government whether at home to preserve skill in industry or possibly abroad after many errors to save our own people from massacre. The world is dangerous. Government must have both the ability and will to act.

37

Nuclear War or Dialogue With the Russians?

ARE we going to blow up the world, including ourselves? — or are we going to reach a reasonable arrangement? This is the stark choice which should be presented to the Russians in a continual international dialogue. Is the risk of nuclear war exaggerated? What is a reasonable arrangement? These are the questions that need discussion. "Nuclear war is highly probable" said recently a Nobel Prize winner who has possibly a longer experience of international negotiations than any man alive. The evidence supports him, for the two power blocks are bumping into each other all over the globe. Some optimists suggest that war might be limited to conventional weapons. But all wars escalate. Who is going to be defeated without using everything he has got wherever and whenever he can? And it is now clear that both sides possess sufficient nuclear weapons to destroy the world. For the first time in history we face the possible end of mankind.

What can we do about it? Certainly not disarm while the Russians remain armed, which is the present tendency. It is suicide to present the other side with the temptation of a pushover. We must always be satisfied that disarmament is mutual. An agreed right of inspection would render this comparatively easy with conventional forces, while modern science may now, or soon, be able to detect any concealment of nuclear weapons. In any case a determined West can use its greater resources and technology to maintain at least a parity which renders war too dangerous for either side.

The question arises: what can be a reasonable arrangement to reduce the risk of war occurring by the chance of accident in some local event, which is now becoming acute? The first and simplified answer is that everyone should mind his own business. Let the world be divided into continental systems or spheres of influence, each containing sufficient foodstuffs and raw materials to afford a good life in a well organised society. For instance, North and South America, Europe and Africa, the Russian communist system, the different Chinese communism, the Far East round Japan, and another system round Iran and India. Each of these areas, with the aid of modern science, would be capable of producing more than the whole world could a few years ago. The future would be settled by proving which system was the best. To any rational mind this must seem better than any attempt to impose a system by force which would mean a war of world destruction.

What would be the chance of anything of the kind being accepted, if seriously proposed by the West in a foreign policy of persisting dynamism? None, if we were so weak in arms that we presented Russia with a pushover to attain at one stroke its aim of world communism. A good chance if it appears that war would mean Russia and its communism would be as dead as ourselves. The old world replies that Russia was always expansionist. They have not noticed the difference presented by modern weapons, or the difference between Czarism and Marxism. To combat any man in politics or to deal with him it is helpful to understand his case and his belief. The real Marxists believe that every other system in the world is going to collapse and that they can then pick up the pieces. They would await that event rather than incur war in which both sides would perish.

The question arises whether Russian communists still believe in Marxism. This proposal would test their belief. Some maintain that Russian communism is approaching economic and political breakdown and would go to war rather than admit collapse. This would indeed be a strange inversion of Marxism which always held that the capitalist powers would go to war before their collapse, and that Russian armaments must be adequate to meet the danger. Their failures in economics and their political difficulties may be evident, but it is unlikely that they are sufficient to break their enormous apparatus of internal control. The risk of destruction in world war must appear greater to the rulers of communism than the risk of internal upheaval, certainly as long as we maintain parity in weapons. In any case let us put these grave issues to the test, which can be the best chance of peace.

Gromyko said recently (27.5.78): "We have no intention of grabbing the whole of Africa, or any part of it. We do not need it." At this announcement our diplomats apparently just sat back blinking, as they did previously when Khruschev offered fourteen times to withdraw from Europe if the Americans would do the same. The reason usually given is that "you cannot believe a word the fellows say." There is nothing new in this, for in international affairs one side seldom if ever believes what the other side says. The point is it should be put to the test of fact, at first in private negotiations and if that gets nowhere, in public debate on world television. One of two things will then occur, either a gain for world peace or a loss to the communist cause by the exposure of its spokesmen as bluffers and liars. It is certain that Russia needs nothing economically from Africa and is just there to win a political advantage at the risk of world war. Sense may intervene now the chance of global disaster appears so imminent. We need a persisting dynamism from a West united in foreign policy and in maintenance of adequate armaments. We need the economic power of united Europe which can place bulk orders for foodstuffs and raw materials with African countries and require any reasonable conditions in return. Above all, we need the political genius of a truly united Europe to hold the balance of the world and so to keep the peace.

38

Mosley Speaks

SPEAKING in London at an Action Society evening on May 19 Sir Oswald Mosley said: It would not have made any difference who won the last election, because the policies of the parties were in reality the same. Their measures were identical, but their members detested each other on personal grounds. Conditions had previously been the opposite. They maintained personal friendships while opposing each other with profoundly different policies. For instance, Churchill had made him a member of his "Other Club" while he was vigorously opposing Churchill's policies in Parliament. Even after the outbreak of war, when he and friends had been thrown into prison without charge or trial because some Labour members of the Government threatened to resign if they were not, he remained on terms of close friendship with some members of the Churchill family. It was recognised that it was possible honourably to differ on great issues. Britain had not yet the values of a banana republic, which took any chance personally and permanently to eliminate an opponent.

Present policies were those of the twenties and thirties, which he had opposed all his life with constructive alternatives. After a recent and disastrous experience of inflation they were simply returning to their old situation. Unemployment to limit or break the power of the trade unions was created by an exaggerated restriction of the money supply. Men walked the streets in unemployment while many others were poor for lack of the goods which they and their idle machines could produce. If the purchasing power of our own people were not so reduced, we were told that we should fail to compete on the markets of the world. We had originally been the first industrial nation, and lived as if we still were. Under the present system we had to sell

Last Words : Broadsheets 1970-1980

about a third of our manufactures on world markets in order to pay for about half our foodstuffs and raw materials, which had to be imported. This had to be done in a world where many nations, large and small, West and East, were all trying at the same time to sell more than they bought; a mathematical impossibility.

In the period of present failure it was vital to keep the contrary idea alive. The people could turn to it quickly when they finally realised the present system would not work. Europe was now being blamed by some people who had entered too late and in the wrong way. To make common market before any measure of common government was to put the cart before the horse. They needed three clearly defined spheres of government, regional, national and European. Each would have a different function and all fear of losing what mattered in their national sovereignty would thus be eliminated.

There would be the extension of patriotism which had occurred at each stage of human development. The Anglo-Saxon kingdoms had come together to make England, which had then joined with Wales and Scotland to make Great Britain. Local patriotism was very strong and should be given full scope. At another level and for different purposes it would be integrated with national and European patriotism. Thus could be solved not only the question of Scottish and Welsh devolution, but the age-old problem of Ireland. North and South would have their own government but would act together in clearly defined spheres at the national and European levels. Europe was the vital factor in maintaining world peace, and could thus become the third super-power capable of holding the balance of the globe.

All too fantastic, some would reply, you always try to do too much, and on occasion he would plead guilty to that charge. Yet great things could only be done in a great way. This was now more than ever proved true by small policies muddling towards great disasters. British politicians had twice recently been saved by the scientists. The discovery of North Sea oil alone had saved their island policies from bankruptcy. The discovery of nuclear weapons had prevented the overrunning of Europe by Russian armies. Politicians could not always rely on scientists to save them. We needed new thought in a new age.

The Empire was gone as a result of the war, and few would prefer what had risen in its place. We had possessed a quarter of the globe, whose development he had always urged as a clear alternative to their international policy. A united Europe was the present alternative. This creation could lead the way to as many as six continental systems: Europe-Africa and the British Dominions, America north and south, Russian communism, Chinese communism, the Middle East with India and Iran, the Far East with Japan. Was all this too big and difficult? Did they prefer muddling on through continual friction to nuclear war with consequent world destruction?

The really practical objection to the great policy now necessary was that Britain under recent governments had become uncompetitive in comparison with other European countries. Sooner or later we should have to squeeze the wind and water out of our national life. During the process of British revival some measure of protection might be needed for British industry. The present enormous volume of manufactured imports could not continue indefinitely. Yet the policies of our insular nationalists would incur a worse disaster. If they used protection to exclude the industries of other nations they would find themselves completely excluded in their own sales abroad on which they were entirely dependent to pay for our imports of foodstuffs and raw materials. A real European policy on the other hand would render possible a temporary protection. Let us say to our European partners: we will enter a three-tier government, regional, national and European, on a definite time-table. We ask you to bear with us in the interval, while we put our house in order behind a temporary protection of industry. Britain was vital to the ultimate Europe, and he believed that such temporary policies would be accepted. It was late, but not too late.

39

The Prospect of Another War

WHEN the possibility of another war arises minds turn inevitably to the two previous tragedies of our times. Many of us were bound together by an overriding interest, the determination to prevent another war. In the first war experience of the trenches and the loss of friends scarred many for life. Certainly my own experience of the trenches and also in the air influenced my whole life course. Never could be forgotten that small band of young airmen in the first year of the war who knew the small band on the other side as intimately as the young men from different nations who go motor-racing today. I was too young to have had this pre-war experience but the others were asking why John should kill Hans or Hans should kill John at the behest of tired and cynical old men who had muddled or intrigued the world into this disaster.

This vast sentiment was reinforced by the simple question of the Second World War. What were we fighting about? We were then confronted by people who did not want anything we had got. We are now confronted by people who want everything we have got. The last thing Hitler could possibly desire was a multi-racial Empire. Such a quest would have rendered ridiculous everything he had ever said. We meet the reply that politicians often do the opposite of what they have said, and this is sometimes true about! The small trickery of current politics! Yet in these major matters it was! Quite impossible for a man who had I rested his whole assault on the basic foible of racialism.

We meet the further reply: Hitler wanted to conquer the world. Pause a moment and consider the military position. Even if their armies had overrun the whole of Europe they would still have

The Prospect of Another War

been confronted with the question of swimming the Atlantic in face of the combined Anglo-American fleets. Anyone insisting on such a plan from the Prussian General Staff would have quickly been certified insane. The weapon balance in hand surely ruled it out. Today the technical situation is entirely changed. Modern weapons can reach the whole world, and anyone with a commanding lead in such means can dominate the earth. Also any considerable exchange of fire by these arms can destroy the world. Yet eminent authority has said recently that nuclear war was 'highly probable'.

Eminent science added that in known time several stars have blown up, and wryly concluded that several civilisations have achieved nuclear fusion. What then can be done about it in face of communism, which unlike fascism desires to possess the world? The latter creed was ultra nationalist and consequently took an entirely different form in different countries with an undue, indeed dangerous lack of interest in other people.

The answer surely is that European and American statesmanship must continuously confront the communist leaders with a direct question. The world can be blown up any day, and it includes ourselves. What are we going to do about it? The answer could be found if the world could be divided for political, military and economic purposes into several continental systems. Within such areas each creed would have the practical opportunity to prove which was the best, and we rest would eventually follow. As we are none of us always right or always wrong in all things we might even learn something from each other.

40

The Fear of Free Speech

Letter in Reply by Oswald Mosley
Refused Publication by the *Sunday Telegraph*

Sir — May I reply briefly to Peregrine Worsthorne's comments on my Olympia meeting in your last issue? Is it seriously contended that our stewards were in the wrong when they overcame with their bare hands men who came to break up the meeting and to attack any defenders with razors and knives? For years previously open meetings had been impossible. The old parties just held ticketed meetings of their own supporters.

Yet free speech is clearly the basis of any free system of government. It should not be defended by 'private armies' in the uniforms necessary to recognise each other in such fighting. They only arise when government has ceased to function.

The first duty of government is to defend free speech. They should give this duty to the police. It should also be a considerable offence in law to deny opponents by the use of violence the right to speak. Those who have the ability to reply in debate will agree with me. My supporters never felt any need or desire to attack the meetings of others.

Yours truly,

Oswald Mosley

www.ingramcontent.com/pod-product-compliance
Lightning Source LLC
Chambersburg PA
CBHW071433160426
43195CB00013B/1887